Sponsored By The Holy Spirit

Sponsored By The Holy Spirit

Gene Burgess

iUniverse, Inc.
New York Lincoln Shanghai

Sponsored By The Holy Spirit

iUniverse books may be ordered through booksellers or by contacting:

iUniverse
2021 Pine Lake Road, Suite 100
Lincoln, NE 68512
www.iuniverse.com
1-800-Authors (1-800-288-4677)

ISBN-13: 978-0-595-35410-8 (pbk)
ISBN-13: 978-0-595-79906-0 (ebk)
ISBN-10: 0-595-35410-6 (pbk)
ISBN-10: 0-595-79906-X (ebk)

Printed in the United States of America

To Heather, my companion and soul mate for more than 40 years. She has endured times of great anxiety and rejoiced in untold blessings.

And to our son, Som (Doyle), and our daughter, Deborah, who grew up under trying circumstances in Southeast Asia. Also to Scott Trulove, who has been a source of happiness to our family, as Deborah's husband. And to my brothers, Ron and Phil, who endured untold agony at my hands, growing up.

Finally, to a host of people who have stood by us and encouraged us in our years of ministry.

Contents

Foreword. xi

Comments By Friends. xiii

Introduction xvii

CHAPTER 1   Sponsored By The Holy Spirit. 1

CHAPTER 2   The Cigar Lady 4

CHAPTER 3   Oil And Water 6

CHAPTER 4   A Lesson About Rattlesnakes 8

CHAPTER 5   Maybe It's Only A Broken Leg 10

CHAPTER 6   Explosion—"Great Balls Of Fire" 12

CHAPTER 7   Special Salt And Pepper Shakers 15

CHAPTER 8   Maybe I'll Be A Baptist—I Believe In Visions 18

CHAPTER 9   Plane Crash 21

CHAPTER 10   The Elvis I Knew. 25

CHAPTER 11   Just Pastor That Sunday School Class 30

CHAPTER 12   May Day And The Scarlet Cord 32

CHAPTER 13   Near Stampede At My First Revival. 37

CHAPTER 14   I Couldn't Let Her Get Away 39

CHAPTER 15   "We Don't Want Any Of Your Medicines!" 44

CHAPTER 16   Burning The Bridge. 48

CHAPTER 17   Outsmarted By A Cat. 51

CHAPTER 18   Confusion In The Hospital 54

CHAPTER 19   Lost In A Canadian Blizzard. 57

CHAPTER 20   Bible Smuggler. 62

CHAPTER 21   Was It A Witch's Curse? 65

CHAPTER 22   "What A Healing Jesus". 92

CHAPTER 23   I'm Glad She Woke Up 97

CHAPTER 24   "Deadly" Pineapple 100

CHAPTER 25   No, He's Not Drunk!. 103

CHAPTER 26   The Bob Morton Story 106

CHAPTER 27   Saved By The Sweet Potato Man 110

CHAPTER 28   "Is This The Last Supper?"—A Cure For The
              Fear Of Flying 112

CHAPTER 29   "I See Brain Tumors In My Practice Every
              Day!" 116

CHAPTER 30   Surrounded By Communist
              Guerillas—Mindanao. 119

CHAPTER 31   Let God Use Anyone He Chooses 122

CHAPTER 32   The Flying Machine & The Nipa Hut On Fire . . . 125

CHAPTER 33   The Crashing Dove 128

CHAPTER 34   She Saw A Snake Attacking 139

CHAPTER 35   "There's Life In Jesus' Name" 142

CHAPTER 36   Uncle Bill Got His Money! 146

CHAPTER 37   I Had Judge Hooks Arrested—A Confession 150

CHAPTER 38   God's Hit Men 153

CHAPTER 39   Bartlett Resurrection 163

ACKNOWLEDGEMENTS

Without the help and encouragement of a core of people, this book would never have been published. Dan Johnson, a noted author, inspired me to begin putting my thoughts into print. Beverly Reinagel accomplished the task of translating my scribbling into a readable format. Amy Tollison invested many hours in editing. Also, the final proof team composed of Dixie Emmons, Dr. Larry and Carol Lacy, Duane and Jeanne Knight, and Hilton Burkholder were invaluable. And finally my wife, Heather, put aside her own plans to sit at the computer for countless days and nights preparing the final document.

FOREWORD

Contrary to the opinion of some people, the ministry is "tough duty." It requires total dedication to the One who called the preacher—that is if you still believe in a "God-called" preacher.

I have known Gene Burgess as a "God-called" preacher for nearly thirty-five years. He came to preach one of his earliest revival meetings for the church I pastored in Milan, Tennessee. As a young man, barely out of college where he had trained to be a pharmacist, there was no denying the touch of God and the call of God upon this fine young man.

Brother Burgess was the product of one of the finest Christian homes in Memphis, Tennessee. His father, Doyle Burgess, was a prince among men and one of the most godly Christians I have ever known. His mother was in a class all by herself as a devoted servant of Jesus Christ.

With a background like that, it wasn't surprising to me that their son, Gene, would feel the call of God upon his life.

This book chronicles the real-life experiences of a young man who sets out to do the will of God, regardless of the forces of darkness that might be arrayed against him. The Burgesses are gentle people who love God and His people with a deep, though quiet passion.

You will not find in these pages words of unproven theory, but the true-life experience of a man and his wife who determined to do the will of God with a whole heart. Their mission was clear to them: tell everybody they could possibly reach that Jesus loves them and will save whosoever comes to Him.

Their ministry has been highly successful based on two outstanding criteria: one, their churches have always grown numerically through evangelistic growth and two, the devil gets stirred up and fights when he loses "territory."

This is a picture of ministry as it really is: a series of battles and victories. Even when they have tasted the bitter brew of rejection, Gene and Heather Burgess never strayed from the call of God. They simply waited on God and found another place to minister. That takes character of the highest order.

If you are a minister, you will find some very familiar scenes in these pages. If you are a "layman," you will discover what it's really like behind the scenes when the minister is out of the pulpit.

This book is meat for men. It is truth with compassion. You will find encouragement to keep fighting the fight of faith here.

As I stated earlier, I have known this author, Gene Burgess, for more than three decades at this writing. I can vouch for his character. He is a man of God and is married to a wonderful woman of God. You will be blessed by this work.

Rev. Gene Jackson
Tennessee District Superintendent
of the Assemblies of God, 1964-2003

COMMENTS BY FRIENDS

I wish to take this opportunity to state that Gene Burgess is a Godsend to Shelby County, Tennessee. He is a master in bringing to Shelby County the reconciliation that is needed between all religions, races, cultures, and political parties.

While he is without question, one of the best educated members of the clergy, his ability to speak in a manner that reaches the most illiterate in society is a characteristic that is needed so badly in this area. He speaks in a manner that evinces a spiritual basis, yet is so practical that even the hardest of hearts can understand what he is saying.

A C Wharton, Jr.
Shelby County Mayor

Gene has touched thousands of lives through his ministry for over forty years. Through accounts of his experiences that are both uplifting and, at times, humorous, I'm glad he has shared his unique experiences in service to God and humanity.

Whether it be the story of how he was called to service in Guam, the time he felt near death on a flight to Dakar, Senegal, or his personal encounter with efforts to end racial segregation in our own country in the early 1960s, he provides riveting, life-changing accounts of his unique experiences.

Any reader of his book will come away with a clear portrait of a dedicated Christian who has had a remarkable journey of discipleship.

William Gibbons
District Attorney General
Shelby County, Tennessee

Dr. Burgess, through an easy reading writing style, has captured the essence of functional Christianity through personal vignettes taken over the course of a 40-year worldwide ministry. The short chapters allow readers to easily digest simple truths that help all of us navigate the trials and tribulations of life using the foundational principles of the Bible and our faith. Our doubts, frailties, strengths and talents are identified by Dr. Burgess who through his personal experiences gives us hope for the future and the promise for a better tomorrow.

Mark H. Luttrell, Jr.
Shelby County Sheriff

I read with great interest the faith walk of Pastor Burgess. What a great example for all of us. Bartlett First Assembly of God is a growing church, and I'm certain that God is using the example of Pastor Burgess to build His Kingdom.

Keith McDonald
Mayor of Bartlett, Tennessee

Rev. Gene Burgess has proven to be a man with a passion for ministry. In both world missions and pastoring, he has seen lives dramatically changed by the power of the gospel. The Tennessee District of the Assemblies of God has been enriched and empowered by his contribution as missionary and pastor. He is a man of vision and integrity and both are evident in the fruitfulness of his ministry.

Robert E. Turner,
Tennessee District Superintendent of the Assemblies of God

Rev. Gene Burgess draws from the experience of many years in the ministry as he shares from his heart about adversity and triumph in obeying the call of God. His experience on the mission field and serving as a senior pastor qualifies him to be heard. You will be richly blessed as you read in his book about the things he has faced and how God has been faithful and honored our brother's ministry.

Rev. Glenn Burks
Executive Secretary/Treasurer
Tennessee District of the Assemblies of God

I have known Gene Burgess for many years. He is a man totally committed to God and delights himself in doing His work.

Early stories of Gene and his two brothers and their boyhood pranks, pharmaceutical school, then evangelist, husband, father and missionary to many parts of the world, will amuse, encourage and bless you as he relates God's hand on his life.

Dr. Thomas H. Lindberg
Pastor, First Assembly of God, Memphis

With personal knowledge of the ministry of Gene and Heather Burgess for more than 40 years, I have found the chapters of ***Sponsored by the Holy Spirit*** to be a very accurate reflection of the vitality and effectiveness of their labor in the Lord's vineyard.

The practical vignettes that are shared in this book are inspiring and encouraging. These testimonies come from a man who has lived through the experiences that demonstrate true spirituality.

Walking by faith leads to being "surprised" by the Holy Spirit at times. Gene Burgess has been willing to walk in very difficult and demanding circumstances and allowed the Holy Spirit to work in and through his life.

Having known Gene Burgess' family for most of his life, I see a faith that once was in his parents, being demonstrated in his life, and established in the lives of his children.

Dr. Robert H. Spence
President of Evangel University, Springfield, Missouri.

I knew and loved Doyle and Mildred Burgess. The names are legendary in business and church circles in Memphis. Their legacy lives on in the ministry of their son, Gene Burgess. Sponsored by the Holy Spirit tells that story. It is at once informative and compelling, as the chapter titles suggest. It is almost impossible to read one chapter without reading them all, and no one will read the book without giving praise to a faithful God Who honors a mother's prayers and a father's example.

Dan Johnson, author and inspirational speaker.

I had the privilege of traveling with my friend, Gene Burgess, in the early days of his preaching ministry. Later we met up on the mission field in the Philippines where he served for many years. I have sung for him numerous times during his pastoral ministry. The Burgess' and Blackwood family's lives have been entwined for many years, and I have always been blessed by his gentleness, meekness and compassion. You will be blessed by the account of his journey with the Lord, for his life truly has been 'sponsored by the Holy Spirit.'

Thanks for mentioning our family in your book. I loved the cat story.

Jimmy Blackwood
Blackwood Brothers Quartet

Few men have been blessed by God with the experiences of life that Gene Burgess has lived. Even fewer are able to link those impressive experiences to the presence of God's Spirit. The stories that he shares weave a picture of God's purpose through tales of adventure, tragedy and humor. Not only are they fun to read; they draw the reader into the presence of God—at work in power in our world.

Al Weir M.D. Author of *When Your Doctor Has Bad News:*Zondervan

INTRODUCTION

Many people have started on the journey to heaven, but are having a "bad trip." This book of short, easy-to-read chapters will inspire you to enjoy your journey.

I am now completing 42 years of full-time Christian service. My passion has not only been to win people to Christ, but to assist them to be all God desires.

The Lord called me from my practice of pharmacy into the ministry in 1963. In the beginning, the task of becoming a traveling evangelist seemed impossible. In fact some said I'd never make it! At times it appeared they were right.

As you read these pages, you will see the evidence of God's mercy and grace working through two ordinary people. And it's my prayer that you'll realize that what God has done through us, He can do through you.

Over the years many people have encouraged us to keep on, and believe that the Lord would see us through some very stormy experiences. One reason I want to help encourage pastors and Christian workers, is that so many have encouraged us. Without them, the journey would have been much rougher.

Both my wife, Heather, and I had the benefit of a stable, loving, Christian home. If you had this advantage, you began life miles ahead of the crowd.

Like my father, I had become a registered pharmacist. Of course I was proud to have my Doctorate of Pharmacy degree on the wall, and serve as an instructor at the University of Tennessee. But an inner desire led me beyond lay ministry into full-time Christian service.

I had no formal Bible training, but a friend, Dr. Robert Ashcroft, encouraged me to be a Bible student for the rest of my life. I embarked on a series of disciplined home Bible study courses from Global University. Years later, I completed a Master's degree at the Assemblies of God Theological Seminary. That degree has opened the door for me to teach Bible school courses in eight former Soviet Republic countries.

For two years, I traveled across the United States alone. Then in 1965, Heather and I were married. We continued on in ministry that carried us to 130 countries. Many stories in the book relate to exciting, humorous, as well as trying events on those journeys. During our six years as evangelists together, we invested two years overseas. Twice, we ministered for a year each, encircling the globe. At times there were bare escapes from death. Several times God graciously healed me during our 14 years of ministry in the Asian tropics.

Our two children, Deborah and Som, shared in many of these adventures. I have intentionally included the names of a number of people you may not know. These are some people who are special to me. They may not all be famous, but they are my heroes and have helped and encouraged me over the years.

1

SPONSORED BY THE HOLY SPIRIT

My hands literally shook as I read the telegram that reached us in Bangalore, India. We had just completed three months of crusade ministry, traveling mainly by train over India, an area the size of Texas. Brushing back the tears, my wife, Heather said, "It's not fair."

A broken promise sent our lives into a tailspin. How can God be glorified when good Christian people do bad things?

This opportunity for "character development" started six months earlier in Tokyo, Japan. At that time our lives had been neatly planned with overseas crusades for a full year, followed by a year booked with crusades in the USA. When the military church in Japan elected us as their pastors, we had reluctantly accepted. Tokyo was congested, expensive and the language seemed impossible. Yet somehow I felt it was important to put all other plans on hold, sensing that we were facing a change in direction. Well, change is what we got.

The church in Tokyo needed us in June, so as we completed the India ministry we cancelled all our other plans. But now, this telegram: "Rev. Burgess, we are sorry to inform you that we have changed our minds. The church has decided to cancel our call to you as pastor, as we know of another man who might fit our needs better." I wondered—how do you get fired before you even start?

So what was next? One door closed—slammed actually. We had cancelled all our crusades and seminars for the next year and a half. We were in the heart of India with a two-year-old baby girl and limited finances.

A storm had blown into our lives. In the turbulence we fell on our knees in desperation. What were we going to do? Where were we to go? Even though I was pretty slim at the time, I even got desperate enough to fast. Some storms can blow you into the arms of Jesus.

Three days later a second telegram arrived. Our Missions Department had an urgent need. "Would you consider going to Guam to serve as interim pastor?" Our immediate response was "Yes." We didn't have a clue where Guam was. Finding a map, we located our new home halfway between Manila, Philippines and Honolulu, Hawaii—the middle of nowhere.

After a 10-hour flight, our plane touched down on the small island at sunset. The cabin door opened and humid heat poured into the plane. *Some celebrity must be on the flight,* I thought, looking at the large crowd waving signs outside. I could see no one, not even in first class, that looked particularly important.

Gathering up our little girl's things, we were the last to exit the plane. "There's Pastor Burgess," someone shouted. As we approached the crowd—what a shock. Most of the guys had shoulder-length hair, and the girls wore bare feet and beach attire. "Jesus People" as some called them, now surrounded us waving scripture placards and shouting, "Praise the Lord." We were suddenly plunged into the most exciting, rewarding time of our ministry. A mighty revival was sweeping Guam!

The Commander of the Naval Base opened his home for these youth. Teens and young adults with guitars crammed into every corner and overflowed into the yard in the evenings. When the gatherings reached more than 50, Commander Gil Boggs turned over the Navy gym to us every Friday night.

The gatherings were more like "happenings,": songs, testimonies, questions, answers, dialogue, Bible study and always powerful prayer. Between this group and the church I had come to pastor, people were being saved almost daily. The monthly baptisms at the local beach were stepped up to twice monthly. When the tide was out, the water was so shallow that we were forced to gather at the center of the public beach, where a World War II bomb crater had left the water deeper. Only once did a policeman stop us to ask for our permit. He found our papers in order, but slightly embarrassed, he told us we would still have to move. When I asked why, he replied that there were some people down the beach having a beer bust, and the songs and testimonies were making them uncomfortable. I turned to the band and declared, "Turn up the volume!"

What wonderful days. No one knows how many young people were saved and filled with the Spirit; there were hundreds. Many were delivered from drugs.

One day, the youth began working on a float for an island-wide parade. Their float was quite good, but the kids were so disappointed to come home without a trophy. Several weeks later, I attended a minister's meeting and noticed a trophy sitting on a table. "Whose is this?" I asked.

"We don't know who to give it to," someone replied. "On the float sponsor's form, all it says is 'Sponsored by the Holy Spirit.'"

I gladly claimed the trophy and took it back to the kids who went wild with cheers and "hallelujahs."

Yes, the darkest hour of our lives was followed by the brightest, and it was "sponsored by the Holy Spirit!"

2

THE CIGAR LADY

They wanted her out of the church. The older "saints" said she was too friendly
with the men, too enthusiastic, overly dressed. And for other "good reasons" they
wanted Pastor Pickthorn to ask her to leave the church.

At this time, the Memphis First Assembly of God had about 100 members
and was located on South Third Street. A core group of ladies seemed to run the
church. Maybe that's why more men didn't attend.

Pastor William Pickthorn was a caring, able man who had brought the church
a long way. He was not one to make a quick decision. This demand would not
only remove one attractive young lady from the church roll, but could so disillu-
sion her with "Christians" that she might stray from God.

The people had no way of knowing what an unstable home she came from.
One typical Christmas morning in Tupelo, Mississippi, her family awoke to find
her stepfather had stolen all their Christmas presents to buy liquor. Such was her
background.

Pastor Pickthorn embarked on some detective work. The young lady in question worked in downtown Memphis at Pantese Drug Store. Abe Plough who also
was the owner of Plough, Inc. that made Coppertone ™ among other things and
was a family friend. He owned this chain of drugstores.

One day the pastor slipped unnoticed into the store. He observed this vivacious girl working at the cigar counter. Long before the days of cancer worries,
she had just accepted selling cigars as part of her job.

A gentleman came in to buy a cigar. But the winsome young lady was so
engaging, that he bought the whole box! Well, the pastor didn't like her selling
cigars, but he just prayed for God's wisdom as he slipped out unnoticed.

Meanwhile, the church was experiencing a spiritual revival. One night as the
altar call was given, there was deep conviction. The minister urged folks to come
forward for salvation. No one responded. Then the cigar lady left her seat. She
spoke to one of the men about giving his life to the Lord. Immediately the man

rushed to the altar. Some gathered to pray with him. Then she noticed another man. She went back and invited him to Jesus; he came forward also. One more time, this vibrant young lady went to a third gentleman. All three men were wonderfully saved. All they needed was a caring person to reach out to them.

Well, that settled the issue. Pastor Pickthorn met with the "kicking-out committee." They again demanded she be dismissed as a church member. Now resolute, the pastor reminded them of the service where she had brought three men to the Lord. Then he asked them a pointed question, "How long has it been since any of you have led a soul to Christ?" Only silence and muttering followed. The issue never came up again.

You ask who was this caring, vivacious young lady? Well, she was my mother, Mildred Sparks Burgess.

The scary thing is this: If my mom, a rather immature Christian, had been rejected by a church she deeply loved, what would have happened to her? She developed into one of the most honored, respected women in the Assemblies of God fellowship nationally. If a few people had had their way, would I have had the benefit of a godly caring mother? It's very doubtful if I would even be serving God today myself.

3

OIL AND WATER

Some think that oil and water will not mix, but that's because they don't know the "rest of the story."

Pastor Hamill seemed agitated. As a seven-year-old, I could be easily intimidated and awed by that man. In fact I was awed by him for the 38 years he was my pastor. Yet beneath the gruff exterior there was really a tender heart.

He boomed, "Somebody spilled water on the altar last Sunday night!" I shuddered. It was I, I had done it again. After service I approached the pastor and explained that it wasn't water but tears. You see, God so melted my heart as a seven-year-old boy, that I had repented of all the big time sins that little fellows could commit. Most of the things that happened at that early age have been forgotten, but I'll never forget that night.

There was a spirit of revival and renewal in the church in the old First Assembly of God on South Third Street. The little church of 100 was booming and God was working.

One Sunday night I couldn't locate my parents. They were usually the last to leave anyhow as they enjoyed visiting after services. But neither could be found. Then someone explained, "I think your dad is in the junior boys Sunday School class." This sounded pretty strange, so I checked it out.

I found Dad underneath a table with his hands uplifted, speaking in some strange language. My very reserved father didn't look very sophisticated for a prosperous pharmacy owner. There was something strange though, so I had to ask, "Who put baby oil on Daddy's face?" Then someone explained that my Dad had received the Baptism in the Holy Spirit similar to what happened in the Book of Acts. He really did shine as God's glory flowed into his life. Some years later I discovered what all of this meant.

My dad became an excited Christian. He began closing the business, Burgess Pharmacy, on Sundays to be in church. The little store at Hollywood and Chelsea prospered despite being open only six days a week. Church was the center of our lives,which was true of Heather's family as well. Dad was elected to the deacon board. He served over 30 years as the church expanded to 1084 East McLemore and in 1961 the church moved to 255 North Highland.

My father was not ashamed of the gospel (Romans 1:16); the Holy Spirit gave him boldness. As three more businesses were added, he still had printed on the bottom of all correspondence, "My main goal in life is to work for God. To earn a livelihood I practice pharmacy."

For 30 years, he led a team to Fort Pillow Prison on the first Sunday of each month. The trip on treacherous two-lane Highway 51 took two hours each way. As I became a lay minister, I enjoyed assisting my dad. The auditorium at the prison was usually filled with 500 hardened inmates. Yet often, about 100 men would be so touched they'd come to the altar for salvation.

Then on the third Sunday afternoon of each month, Mom assisted by Dad and myself, would lead a service at the Crippled Adults Hospital. Each service would close with the song "God Be With You Till We Meet Again." By the next gathering, some had gone on to meet the Lord.

Dad suffered a massive heart attack at age 32. He never fully recovered. In those days there were no miracle drugs, no coronary bypasses, and heart balloons were unheard of. Every few years, a call would come, "Dad's had another heart attack, we're not sure he'll make it."

Yet in spite of his heavy workload and diminished energy, he kept pushing. For over 20 years he traveled all over Tennessee as an unpaid director for the Men's Ministries. He knew that men are the keys to building God's work.

As we left the Memphis airport in 1975 for our missionary assignment in the Philippines, I can still see Dad. He held two-year-old Som in his arms and five-year-old Debbie by the hand. We understood it would probably be the last time Dad would see the kids.

Two years later, at midnight, our phone rang. Dad was critical! Three men at our home church bought my ticket to return. My how our lives have been blessed by caring people.

But I have one regret. As Dad lay in the Baptist ICU unit, we lightly joked about playing golf together when he got out. So we never really had a serious talk about life and death. Even though I told him how much I loved him and respected him, I just wish we had connected more closely while growing up.

4

A LESSON ABOUT RATTLESNAKES

The Oklahoma panhandle is rattlesnake country. People have to be careful where they walk. Each year, some die from deadly snakebites.

My Aunt Mary was afraid that I, being a youngster from the city, wouldn't know what a snake looked like. She, wisely or not, proceeded to try and find a rattler so I'd be aware. She had no idea of the surprise that awaited us.

Each summer from the time I was six years old until ten, I went out to visit Aunt Mary and Uncle Jess in Oklahoma. My folks would take me down to Derrick's Shoe Store to get cowboy boots to protect me from the rattlers. Then they'd put me aboard the "rocket train" from Memphis to Amarillo, Texas. My Aunt and Uncle didn't have any children so they were delighted to drive all the way from Guymon, Oklahoma down to Amarillo to get me for two months. Uncle Jess had vast wheat fields as far as you could see.

I was only six when Aunt Mary took me for the snake lesson. Down by the chicken house, she thought we might find a rattler. Sure enough, we did. When my aunt saw the coiled snake, she screamed and took off for the house. Halfway to the house, she realized she'd forgotten something—me. I was fascinated by the curious rattling sound. She ran back, grabbed me and the story ended well. This event has often been recounted at family reunions.

Summer was exciting. By the time I was eight I could ride ole Vick. Vick was a huge working horse on the ranch. I can still recall galloping across the pasture, scaring the steers, and my Aunt Mary screaming at the top of her lungs, "Slow down Gene, be careful!"

Summer was harvest time. We would go into town to hire extra combines and a crew. Long rows of combines would line the road next to the grain elevators. When you "hired a crew," you were expected to provide lodging and meals for them. Many nights these men would sit around the dinner table, their sun-baked faces glowing as the light from the kerosene lamp danced on their features. Then they'd return to the fields to work by their tractor lights.

The ripened harvest was very vulnerable to seasonal hail and heavy downpours. So there was not only excitement, but also anxiety in the air. The Bible has much to say about the harvest being like men who need Jesus. We should have a sense of urgency to share our faith while we still have time.

Almost every day I was out in the wheat field with my Uncle Jess. One day it almost cost me my life. It was fun to sit on top of a whole truckload of golden grain. On that day as we drove to the grain elevator to dump our load, I rode all the way on top of the wheat. At the elevator, the back of the truck opens so the grain can pour out. Uncle Jess thought that it was safe enough for me just to hold onto the side of the truck while the wheat poured out the back. But at age six, I was frightened as the grain moved by my feet and out the back. I let go of my hold and immediately I was sucked under the vast load of wheat. My uncle turned to see what had happened to me. Then someone shouted, "Maybe he's been sucked under the load!" Uncle Jess began to dig feverishly down into the wheat. As you can guess since I'm writing, he found me. Wheat was down in my throat, in my nose and in my ears. I was very frightened, but okay. That was my last ride to the grain elevator.

When it was time for school to start, I returned home each year full of stories of snakes and other danger-filled adventures of farm life.

5

MAYBE IT'S ONLY A BROKEN LEG

"Maybe it's only a broken leg." That's what I told the fireman about my cousin Jimmy Sparks.

Jimmy was six months older than I. He'd lived much of his life with my mother's mom. At about age 10, he joined our family. Now Mom had four "sweet" boys.

Jimmy was even more adventurous and daring than I was. His life hadn't been too happy. His dad drank pretty heavily and had been married "several times," no one was sure how many.

Our ages were close, and we were close. Long bike rides, Boy Scout camp, football in the park across the street, were some of the good times we had.

On a rare occasion my folks would allow us to stay home alone at night while they went out to church. We were forbidden however, to go outside. Yet each time they left, Jimmy would jump on his bike and would hang out with the neighborhood kids.

One Wednesday we were blessed to find a stray puppy. Our folks let us have it. But we couldn't abandon him to go to church, so our parents let us stay home that Wednesday night and care for the little pup. We were warned, "Don't dare leave the house." Well, they hadn't been gone long when Jimmy jumped on his bike.

Just a few moments passed when we heard a fire engine leaving the station near our home. The sirens pierced the night. Finally, the fire truck passed right by our home. I'll never forget the terror that gripped me. It seemed the giant red engine literally shook the house. But in a few moments, the wailing siren died to a moan and stopped.

I could still see the flashing red lights from our living room window when the doorbell rang. "It's Jimmy! He's been hit by the fire truck!"

I ran down the street only four houses away. "Where is Jimmy?" I asked in panic. The fireman seemed dazed and some of the women were crying. That's when I saw Jimmy under the fire truck. "Quick," I ordered. "Get him out. Maybe his leg is only broken." My demands were greeted with silence. Then I took a closer look, which I've long regretted; giant wheels were resting on his body.

My Mom took it especially hard. Our whole family was crushed. The church on McLemore was packed. Our Scout Troop 90 sat together for Jimmy's funeral. Jimmy was decked out in his brand new Boy Scout's uniform.

Marie Brown (Harrup) reminded me of something that had happened just a few days before the tragedy. There had been a great outpouring of the Holy Spirit in our 12-year-old youth class. Jimmy, along with most of us, made a fresh commitment to God. We knew he was ready for this last ride.

Still to this day, I shudder when a fire truck with blaring sirens and roaring motor passes close.

With the loss of my closest friend, I was drawn to Ron Blackwood. His parents, R.W. and Elaine Blackwood, took me to their home after the funeral for several days. They just wanted to be a comfort and help to our family. The Blackwood Brothers had just moved to Memphis a few months earlier. The bonding of the Burgess and the Blackwood families would extend for two generations. Many adventures lay ahead.

6

EXPLOSION—"GREAT BALLS OF FIRE"

Jerry Lee Lewis with his "Great Balls of Fire" had never seen anything like this! A "BOOM" shook the house—an explosion, fire and smoke. Did you ever try to do something nice or creative and have it blow up in your face, literally!

One Saturday afternoon our Boy Scout patrol went to the Alexander's home. Elbert Alexander had been a major in a tank company in World War II. Now retired, he was wonderfully supportive of us boys.

We were at the Alexander's home preparing for another camping trip only a week away. I faced the camping trip with a bit of excitement and also some dread. Almost every time we went camping, some big disaster happened. In my scouting experience that covered six years, nothing ever went as planned. We were part of the problem—we were a bunch of goof-offs and interested in inventing fun rather than learning anything. Doing things the right way seemed boring.

Our Troop 90 was sponsored by our home church, First Assembly of God at 1084 E. McLemore in Memphis. At age 11, I earned my first rank—"Tenderfoot." Over the next 3 to 4 years I climbed through the ranks of 2nd Class, 1st Class, Star, and at age 17, I was a Life Scout. In later years, I wished I had taken the final step to reach the highest Scouting award—Eagle. When I reached the rather high rank of Life Scout, I had earned 15 merit badges.

The Scout Master wasn't too pleased, as the rest of the troop had hardly advanced in rank at all. The leaders enlisted me to help the boys advance and put my plan for Eagle Scout aside. They promoted me, however, to be the Junior Assistant Scout Master. All of a sudden I was a leader of 30 boys and my knowledge was rather limited. The Scout Master thought I knew a lot more than I did.

On one famous campout we had to hike across country. I really thought that I could read a compass. But something went wrong. Maybe the compass was broken. With me as the fearless leader, we all were lost. For several hours we trudged

12

through the hills and the forest, until finally we found a road and got back to camp.

On another day, to earn our hiking merit badge, we had to walk 15 miles. All of us had started out together, but pretty soon we were rather scattered enroute to Camp Courier, Mississippi. At the end of a long hot day, exhausted, we dragged ourselves into the campground. But two boys were missing.

Did this have to be my fault again? Before long a sheriff's car drove up. In the back seat were our two lost sheep. They looked petrified.

They had a right to be scared. Earlier as we were walking, they had forgotten their water canteens. When they saw a house, they walked off the road and up to the house to get a drink. The water hydrant refreshed them but the house looked abandoned.

A bright idea struck them. "Since no one lives here, why don't we test our rock throwing skills at the windows?" In only 20 minutes they had honed their skills and had broken every single window in the house. Just as they completed the contest, the owners drove up. They caught them red handed, and called the sheriff.

I was beginning to learn the perils of leadership. The entire troop was disgraced by two guys who really weren't mean, just city boys out in the country. But part of the blame rested on me, as I should have been able to keep 20 boys in a nice line for 15 miles.

By the way, the two were expelled from the troop. One of the boys, however, became a great athlete and ended up playing pro football for the New York Jets.

But maybe the most exciting experience of my leadership was this summer day at Major Alexander's home. All good Boy Scouts had to learn how to waterproof their matches. Then if it rained, you could start a fire with dry matches.

In order to waterproof matches, we melted bars of wax on their kitchen stove. While they were melting, all of us got under a big shade tree outside where I taught them safety in camping skills. You know, it was kind of like the blind leading the blind. But someone said, "In the land of the blind, the one eye is king!"

Suddenly we smelled smoke. Then we all saw it—a fire in the kitchen. As we rushed in we saw the wax was on fire, and the flames were leaping up 3 or 4 feet high. About then, I wished I were somewhere else.

I knew that water would not help at all but only make things worse. It came to my mind that baking soda was the best fire retardant. Proud of my quick thinking, I yelled for Leon Alexander to hurry and get some. But none could be found. Now some ingenuity had to be employed.

Since baking soda was white, and not available, I reasoned that flour might smother the blaze just as well. Ah, genius at work! Quickly I grabbed a five-pound sack of flour and dumped the whole thing on the blaze.

That's when it happened. My response seemed perfectly logical, but the flour caused a loud booming explosion. Fire danced all around me. The blast blew flaming bits of flour all over the entire kitchen. All of the paint burned off the walls, and the stove was wasted, covered in burning flour and oozing wax. Aside from my hair being singed, I was unhurt except for my pride. All of us were in shock, especially the kid whose house was nearly destroyed.

Now was the time to act calm and in control, though I was shaking on the inside. So I politely thanked Leon for the use of his house, but suggested that we probably would not be meeting there again for a while.

As we left the house, Leon stared speechless—guess he was in shock. Now I had to get ready for the fall-out. The whole bizarre fiasco was totally due to my stupidity. Too bad there was no one else to blame.

I could picture Major Alexander and his wife returning home. There would be Leon, still in shock, and when they would see their kitchen demolished, I knew they'd be on the phone to my father. I was sure I would hear them scream five miles away.

I waited in terror for the phone to ring all that Saturday night. Then I knew that Major Alexander would certainly tell my dad at church next Sunday morning about my great leadership skills and the waterproof match incident.

To my great surprise, he never said one word to the adult scout leader, my dad or me. And since he didn't talk, I didn't mention it until years later. It is hard to comprehend that the Alexanders treated me so well in the years ahead. The little "accident" never was mentioned.

This man showed the love and mercy of Jesus to me. With a chuckle, I still recall this incident and I thank God for gracious people. Then it reminds me to "lighten up" on others when they also "mess up."

7

SPECIAL SALT AND PEPPER SHAKERS

Being the oldest son is not always easy. For one thing, when you are the first born, your parents "practice" on you. Their energies are focused on you to be certain that you turn out all right—whatever that means. My brother Ron joined our family four years following me, and then came Phil in another three years.

At one point, I was the undisputed boss over my two younger brothers. As they grew older, we were more competitive. War games were great ways to entertain ourselves.

Why my dad ever bought us Red Ryder BB guns, I'll never know. But I sure am glad. Guess he really didn't know us too well after all.

If we played cowboys and Indians, I had to always be the cowboy with a BB gun. My brothers were armed with rather harmless bows and rubber tipped arrows. I guess BB's hurt. Because I was the one firing, and my brothers were running through the neighborhood screaming, I didn't "feel their pain."

Our fun came to an abrupt halt one day. I had Ron "treed" on top of the house. He really could scream like a Comanche Indian as he dodged most of the pellets. The neighbors heard the commotion and with horror saw Ron on the roof. So they called the police. After that, my dad confiscated our firearms.

Years later my mother had the house redecorated, but she refused to replace several windowpanes with BB holes made by her "precious" boys. At the time of the damage though, we were not considered very precious.

But being smart and creative, we invented other fun games. Shoe fights in the living room (while my parents were out) were great fun. It required great skill not to hit one of Mom's lamps or the vase, radio, or TV. Unfortunately, there were a few bad shots, and the rest of the evening was spent with a tube of glue—and a prayer that Mom wouldn't notice the cracks.

On one memorable night, Ron kept popping his head up from behind the couch, taunting, "You can't get me!" Then I let loose with a shoe just as his darling head appeared. He got "You can't...," and the shoe popped him right between the eyes! Blood began to flow, and Phil and I tried out our first aid skills. All was well when our folks returned home and found their three little angels ready for bed.

When it came to chores, Dad made me the job foreman, whether it was dusting endless shelves in the drug store or caring for our large yard. It was my job to see that Ron and Phil helped me keep the yard immaculate. Unfortunately, my younger siblings' work ethics were rather meager at ages nine and six. But my dad believed the entire Bible, especially the verse that says, "A man who does not work should not eat."

We had an old-fashioned push mower. Dad said only spoiled, lazy kids had power mowers, which were rather new to the market then. It was August, and the thick Bermuda grass was tough. Ron refused to rake and Phil was really too young to slave, so he guarded the television set. I tried to explain to Ron that if he didn't help me, a terrible accident might happen to him. Now, I don't know why he was concerned since we never fussed or fought much.

Anyhow, Ron jumped on his bike to escape. This wasn't unusual when Father ordered yard work. But when he didn't come back in an hour or two, we did get concerned.

When Dad came home and Ron hadn't returned of course, I couldn't admit I had threatened him with strangulation. When it did get dark and Ron had been gone four or five hours, we all were worried sick. We really did pray for Ron's safety.

Then the phone rang—it was Ron. His voice sounded weak. He was calling from a gas station near Somerville, Tennessee. Ron had ridden his bike on the edge of a two-lane highway 40 miles from our home in Memphis.

Dad went to pick him up. Ron had taken with him his life savings and with that he purchased a "peace offering" for Dad. When Dad arrived, the little guy handed him a sack and collapsed in the back seat. On arriving home, Dad opened his gift—a pair of salt and pepper shakers, two outhouses labeled "I'm full of S" and "I'm full of P." My very sophisticated, proper father proudly displayed these by his desk for over 20 years until he died. Ron now has them as priceless mementoes.

As my brothers eventually grew taller and more muscular than I, I'm so thankful that they didn't totally exterminate me, which I deserved. Today, both Ron and Phil have become successful in their professions. So I may have helped them learn to love work. Of course, I don't deserve all the credit for their accomplishments.

8

MAYBE I'LL BE A BAPTIST—I BELIEVE IN VISIONS

With a bit of frustration I declared, "Maybe I'll be a Baptist!"

Now the Southern Baptist denomination is one of the finest groups in the world. Their influence has helped create the "Bible-Belt" in the South. I've always admired and respected them. The Assemblies of God and Baptist doctrines are similar.

One point of diversion, however, is that the Assemblies of God teaches that after salvation there is another experience that empowers believers. This "enduement of power," as is noted in the Book of Acts, is exemplified by the initial physical evidence of speaking in tongues.

As a teen I had seen the mighty impact of the Holy Spirit Baptism on other people. But I had a problem. I was one of the leaders in our youth group, yet I was one of the few "hard cases." I had sought, prayed, begged and claimed this experience. Nothing happened! So rather than being thought of as a second class Pentecostal at age 16, I just thought of joining the Southern Baptists.

That summer, my dad allowed me a week off from the drugstore if I'd go to the Bethesda youth camp near Nashville. I knew pressure would be exerted on me at camp to receive this experience. But I couldn't pass up the week off with a youth group from First Assembly.

As usual, Aunt Nell Brewer drove us there and served at the camp as chief cook. Aunt Nell, along with Uncle Jack had been the safety net for our family after my mom and dad were married. Much of my early childhood was spent at her "farm" near Millington while my folks worked long hours in the pharmacy. Later when Dad had a bad heart attack, the three Burgess boys and Jimmy Sparks plus some other kids, joined the Brewers' and their children, Eddie and Shirley, at their Fite Road home.

We never got bored or in much trouble at Aunt Nell's. Well, one afternoon the six of us did get in a little trouble. I took her huge butcher knife and played Tarzan in the big field next to her house. I led the troops to cut trails all through the "forest." That night the sheriff came to the house. Being city boys, we didn't realize that we had nearly totally destroyed a half-acre of the neighbor's corn. We hid under the bed, but Aunt Nell as usual worked her magic and they did not put any of us in jail.

Well, I guess there was one other major trial of Aunt Nell's patience. That was when we were robbing the refrigerator in her absence. We did not notice her white cat climbing half way into the refrigerator sniffing out potential snacks. So when I slammed the refrigerator door, that was the end of poor kitty. We all cried, because not only had we killed the cat, but also because Aunt Nell could really throw a fit when she got upset.

As we began to plan our next move, we decided the only spiritual thing to do was to give the cat a good send-off with an appropriate funeral. I served not only as the grave-digger, but the preacher. So when Aunt Nell arrived home, the whole bunch of us were on our best behavior. Before long she began to look for the cat. All we could think of was to ask her if she would come out to the back yard. There we showed her the freshly dug grave site. This may seem amusing to some, but we really were sad. And we were right, she did throw a major fit.

Aunt Nell was a deeply spiritual person, and we loved to ride with her to the annual church camp, singing the whole way. The church services at youth camp were always good in spite of the crude benches and the summer heat. But that summer I was worried that at the prayer time people were probably going to lay hands on me and "help me" receive the Holy Spirit. The normal routine was for one person to shout, "Hang on," while one on the other side encouraged, "Let go."

So I found a quiet corner and prayed alone. I just told the Lord I didn't care if I ever spoke with tongues or had the joy others had. I just sought more of God's presence in my life. That's when something life-changing happened.

The next thing I remember, two hours later I heard someone say, "He's coming around." Aunt Nell was bending over me. At age 16, I had an unforgettable encounter with God. I had often prayed that if I ever received this experience, it would be so dynamic that I would never doubt or question it, or be the same again. I got my desire and more.

Rarely since 1955 have I spoken of what happened, as it was so special, sacred, and personal. I had a vision! In the Spirit, I was transported to some Middle Eastern country. The people were olive-skinned and wore long robes with headdresses. I felt an urge to preach Jesus to them. The Arabic-appearing crowd listened intently in the vision. It must have been a lengthy sermon, as I was "carried away in the Spirit" for over two hours. Because this encounter was so sacred, I didn't speak about it much. But I immediately noticed a new joy, a "holy boldness" for God, and a desire to please the Lord. The Holy Spirit does produce good fruit.

When I returned home, I announced that I wouldn't be a Baptist after all. At the time, the full meaning of this vision was unclear. But six years later, halfway around the world, I understood the full impact of what God did at Bethesda Youth Camp. That story may be found in chapter 15.

9

PLANE CRASH

It had been a great day at Maywood swimming pool. Several from the church, including my closest friend, Ronnie Blackwood, had been there all day. I left just in time to run home and get ready for Wednesday night prayer meeting. The Burgess bunch almost never missed any church services. But this would be a shocking evening,

The Blackwood Brother's Quartet had moved to Memphis in 1950 from Shenandoah, Iowa. Even though they were mainly Church of God in background, they chose First Assembly of God, as it was the leading Pentecostal Church in the city. Gospel quartet music was at its prime. As a 12-year-old boy, traveling the country and singing to large crowds seemed exciting to me.

Periodically, I spent the night with Ronnie Blackwood and I would go with his dad, R.W., down to WDIA where the quartet did live radio broadcasts. In fact, most weekends I was either at Ronnie's house or he was at my house. We were so different. Ronnie had a black belt in karate and he boxed in the Golden Gloves. He was a real dare devil. I was much more reserved, but I enjoyed fun too.

Many Friday nights after our Boy Scout Troop 90 met, Ronnie would come home with me. The bus ride from McLemore took over an hour to our house. Then there was the scary four-block walk in the dark from the bus stop to our house. I could almost see bad guys hiding in the bushes, so when alone I ran top speed. When Ronnie was with me, we just strolled. It does make a difference if you have protective company in scary places.

In funeral services over the years, I've used the analogy to Psalm 23: "I will fear no evil for Thou art with me." The truth is, when we walk through the valley of the shadow of death, we don't fear. Why is that? Because Jesus is there to comfort and protect. Ronnie provided that protection for me.

It's amazing anyone would come home with me on a Friday night. That's because we had to catch the bus by 7 a.m. on Saturday to "work" in one of my dad's four drugstores. Well, work may be stretching it a bit. We did manage to make work fun.

Once we were assigned to dust every bottle in the prescription department. There were hundreds. While I was dusting the "stronger ammonia water" a bright idea flashed into my mind. Ron had been acting devilish, which was rather normal. So I called to him, "Ron, come check this out. Boy this really smells great!"

This ammonia is ten times stronger than what you buy in the grocery store. Ron took a deep breath and collapsed on the floor. He couldn't scream much as he was struggling to breathe. But it sounded like he was trying to say something like "I'll kill you!"

Another Saturday, we were dropped off at my dad's drug warehouse. It was a stifling summer day and we didn't even have a fan. Finally, lunch break came. We went under the viaduct on Jackson Avenue. Ron began throwing rocks at my feet and legs. They really hurt, so I screamed at him. My agony just inspired him to keep it up. Maybe he was getting even with me for the ammonia incident?

Finally, I threatened, "If you don't stop, I'm going to find a rock and hit you right between the eyes." He really thought that was funny as another rock found its mark on my shin. So I got a rock and aimed it for his knees but missed. You guessed it, I got him right between the eyes. Blood gushed over his face. He suddenly stopped laughing as we tried to stop the blood. The gash required several stitches. Soon, Ron's eyes were almost swollen shut. Well, I must admit, I giggled a bit—he looked a mess.

That night, I was to go to Ronnie's house. I didn't know it, but when we got to his home, the Quartet had arrived back in town. Mr. Blackwood—R. W.—was in the house. He would see what I had done to his "precious son." R. W. was my idol. Oh what a powerful baritone voice he had, and he was such a comic.

Sure enough, when we walked in, there stood R. W. Immediately, I apologized to him for cutting Ron's eye. His response was a shocker, "I know Ron and I'm sure he deserved it!" The matter was settled.

R. W. was the pilot of the Blackwood Brother's twin-engine aircraft. For years, the Quartet traveled in a nice Cadillac limousine, but five men trying to sleep on a long trip was tough. And then, they had the records (back before the days of tapes and CD's) filling a trailer they pulled behind.

R.W. was a daredevil and that's where Ron got some of his adventurous spirit I guess. Flying was a natural for R.W. Quickly he progressed through the classes and began to pilot larger and larger aircraft.

Another friend, Billy Barron, had a dad who was a pilot with American Airlines. He knew the plane R. W. flew and Captain Barron was very concerned about their lack of experience with such a large aircraft. But by flying, they could get to the next concert quickly. Anything to beat the Statesmen Quartet. Hovie Lister and his quartet were the Blackwood's dearest friends and also their greatest rivals. The big challenge each night was to see who could steal the show.

Finally, the Blackwoods got that once-in-a-lifetime opportunity. They appeared on the Arthur Godfrey Talent Scouts in New York City on national television. R. W. flew the plane to New York.

The song they chose was "Have You Talked To The Man Upstairs?" Its theological base may have been a bit weak, but the New York audience went wild. The quartet won, and then appeared with top stars each morning for a week in New York. They were able to sing and share their faith. It appeared nothing could stop them, and each of them was only in his mid thirties—the prime of life.

I'll never forget that Wednesday night when our family walked into church. What a shocking scene. People weren't really praying. They seemed to be wailing in agony. Something terrible must have happened.

We found out there had been a plane crash. The Blackwoods had been down in Clanton, Alabama on June 30th,1954. The wind currents were unpredictable, and the runway was unusually short. They removed all the cargo. Only R. W. the pilot, and Bill Lyles the golden bass and co-pilot, took the plane up for a test flight. They were going to have to take off later after dark on an unlighted runway. All seemed to be going well, when suddenly the plane went out of control. There was a fiery crash.

The crowd of quartet admirers began to sob. Beside the runway were James Blackwood, Bill Shaw, and Jack Marshall. One of the men had to restrain James who tried to rush to the smashed blazing wreckage. R. W. and Bill were burned beyond recognition. James Blackwood had to identify them by the newly engraved diamond rings they had bought to commemorate their victory just days before with Arthur Godfrey.

To me and many at First Assembly, these men were not stars but caring, talented Christian gentlemen. Elaine Blackwood and Ruth Lyles were shattered. It was months before they began to function somewhat normally.

Ellis Auditorium, the site of the funeral for R. W. and Bill, was jammed to capacity. I don't know how the Statesmen Quartet could sing. Pastor Hamill felt this loss very deeply but he ministered well.

Bill Shaw, the tenor, rode with my family to the cemetery. The families had asked my dad to make all the funeral and cemetery arrangements. When people are 35 and in their prime, this would be the last thing you would think could happen to them.

I remember James Blackwood sobbing that he'd never sing again. This was one of the deepest pains I've had in my entire life.

This was a crisis for the Quartet. Would they quit or go on? James called the three remaining members together. He told them it was all over if they cancelled the next date, but R. W. and Bill would want them to continue. I can still picture them climbing into James' new Lincoln for the 500-mile drive to Dallas, Texas.

It would only be a few months until they added the legendary bass, J. D. Sumner, and young baritone, Cecil Blackwood. Their inaugural outing was at our church, First Assembly in Memphis. Sincere prayer was offered for them as new voices and personalities were added.

In various combinations, James and Cecil would travel and sing for the next 40 years. Both men would receive the highest award in gospel music. Now both of them have superceded this—they've reached their final destination. Their biggest reward was not on nationwide television, but came when they heard the words, "Well done good and faithful servant."

10

THE ELVIS I KNEW

A brand new pink Cadillac pulled into the parking lot. Standing at the windows of our Sunday School class, we saw Elvis emerge from this beautiful vehicle. Immediately we said to each other, "Oh no, I bet he's in trouble now. Do you think he stole it?"

Elvis was certainly different in a lot of ways. He wore long sideburns. His shopping was done at Lansky Brothers on Beale Street in Memphis, who catered mainly to black clientele. But he was a rather quiet and shy, withdrawn young man.

Our family got acquainted with Elvis a few years before he acquired the pink Cadillac. His dad was an unemployed truck driver at the time. Elvis was a young teenage boy who would ride First Assembly's bus. A couple of times, my dad and I went to the government housing project at Lauderdale Courts to take them groceries.

For several years, Elvis was quite faithful to church and Sunday school. But then I noticed he began to miss. One Sunday as the boys were chatting out in the hallway, his Sunday school teacher walked up. Bill Haltom was one of the finest men and finest teachers any boys' class could have. "We sure have missed you lately," Bill said.

Quickly, Elvis replied, "Haven't you heard? I've gotten a new job; it's a great opportunity. I'm singing in some of the nightclubs on Friday and Saturday nights. Since I get in pretty late, it's hard to get up on Sunday morning."

Bill seemed shocked. Elvis seeing the disappointment quickly added, "Now Brother Bill, you don't have to worry about me. I don't drink or smoke. But the money is so good, I couldn't pass it up." That was 1954.

None of us thought Elvis could sing. But we did know he could wiggle. In fact, it was his wiggle that kept him from being accepted in a church quartet of other young men. This would later be a real joke, as some of these guys struggled to survive while Elvis became world famous. More about that later.

We asked Elvis what songs he sang, because we didn't believe he had earned the money for that new Cadillac. "'That's All Right Momma' is one of my biggest songs." Then we were sure of it. He had stolen that car!

It wasn't long, however, until we began to hear his songs on the radio. Sam Phillips, owner of Sun Studio, had brought together Jerry Lee Lewis, Carl Perkins ("Blue Suede Shoes"), Johnny Cash, and Elvis. Rock and Roll was born on Union Avenue in Memphis July 5, 1954. Some call it, "The sound heard around the world." Others have agreed, "Rock was the message and Elvis was the messenger."

After those hits, we rarely saw Elvis. Soon it was Hollywood; then the purchase of Graceland Mansion. Next to the White House, this is still the most visited home in America today.

Then one Easter evening, Elvis showed up at church. With him, were ten others. A couple were Hollywood stars, along with his bodyguards affectionately called "The Memphis Mafia."

Now I don't want to infer that I was a big buddy to Elvis. But I did know him casually and chatted with him again that evening. "Why don't you come see me at Graceland?" he asked me. I told him that the Lord had called me into full-time ministry, and I was rarely home anymore. Of course he was rarely home either, but I was very impressed by his invitation.

I had been out to visit a couple of times when Elvis first made it big. But a few weeks later, I went out again. The big wrought iron gate was closed and a guard stood in front. When I told him I had an appointment with Elvis, he already knew it but said, "I'm sorry Elvis cannot see you." Just then, as I was standing by the huge gate, three cars screeched to a halt by my side. They were filled with wild looking revelers. The gate swung open for them, but I wasn't admitted.

I knew one of Elvis's guards, who often would visit my dad's drugstore. So when I happened to meet him again, I asked him, "What was the deal? Do you know why I was turned away?"

Rather sheepishly he answered, "Yes, I told Elvis you were down at the gate, and he replied that the party had gotten quite rough and he felt embarrassed for anyone who had known him at church to see what was going on in his house."

Not long after that, Elvis's mom, Gladys, passed away. She was the dearest thing to Elvis. He took it very, very hard. In the months ahead, his dad, Vernon, began to date. Elvis was not too happy about this.

Later, I dropped by my dad's drugstore. Again, I saw one of Elvis's guards sitting at the soda fountain. He commented, "Hey Elvis said he wants you to come out and see him again."

This time, there was no party. But once again, the message came back from the mansion, "Elvis isn't having company!" A few days later I found out the reason. That afternoon, Vernon told Elvis he was going to remarry. Elvis went into a wild rage. A friend told me it wasn't pretty. So that's why there was no company. After that, I was never invited again.

A lot of interesting people came into my dad's pharmacy at 4308 Macon Road in Memphis. One afternoon, a guy with dark, messy hair came in. He had a child by each hand. I noticed he was driving a fancy new Cadillac. He asked for some paregoric. This highly addictive medication contains a bit of opium, but is good for colic and other stomach problems. Under Tennessee Law at the time, you could purchase a half-ounce every 48 hours without a prescription. But each purchaser had to sign a register.

When I asked him to sign, he exclaimed "Don't you know who I am?" When I seemed unsure, he replied with his famous line, "I'm Johnny Cash!" From that time on, Johnny would phone the pharmacy for various items. So periodically, I'd deliver them to his mansion, and yes, he was a generous tipper.

Elvis Presley became a household name. His following was almost cult-like. It's bewildering; he'd buy Cadillacs for strangers, but wouldn't even buy church bonds from my dad as we started the new building on Highland. My father was the last Sunday school teacher he had before he was drawn into Hollywood.

For Elvis, traveling soon got old. Even with all the luxury, he got tired of moving night after night from concert to concert. His manager, Tom Parker was called "50% Parker" because he got half of what Elvis earned. He negotiated long-term contracts at casinos in Las Vegas for Elvis. Elvis's weird life style continued—two or three shows a night, to bed with sleeping pills at sunup, sleep all day, and arise in early evening with pep pills in time for the evening shows.

Elvis idolized the Blackwood Brothers. He'd often sneak backstage into their concerts. He invited Terry Blackwood and the Stamps Quartet with J. D. Sumner to come live in Las Vegas. Terry was a dear friend of mine and was a deeply committed Christian. His dad, Doyle Blackwood, was a very close friend of my father's, Doyle Burgess—the two Doyles.

At any rate, Terry saw the Las Vegas invitation as a true opportunity for ministry. Elvis kept his promise to allow the Quartet a portion of each concert in the casinos to sing gospel songs. Terry reported, "We sang to thousands of people who would never go to church. Sometimes people would approach us and ask for prayer."

Also, in most concerts, Elvis would sing some gospel songs. I believe it gave him a feeling of being close to God. It reminded him of his roots. And perhaps it salved his conscience.

Yes, it had been a long time since Elvis first announced that he had contracts to sing in nightclubs. I'll never forget his comment, "Don't worry about me, I'll never drink or smoke."

Dixie Locke Emmons has given several interviews about her two-and-a-half year courtship with Elvis. They met at our home church. It seemed like the real thing as they went to the junior high prom together. Then Elvis recorded, "Blue Moon of Kentucky," and "You Ain't Nothing But A Hound Dog," and many others. Dixie reports after that, everything changed. "I'd given my heart to the Lord and Elvis was doing things our church didn't approve of. I couldn't go with him to the clubs where they served alcohol." She has no regrets. "A part of me thinks if I'd just hung in there, he'd still be alive, and singing gospel music. But then I think I might have ended up taking some kind of substance to survive the entertainment world."

Growing up, Elvis had numerous godly people encouraging him. Every Sunday as our high school Sunday school class was ready to dismiss, Betty Zschigner Johnson would lead us in repeating Psalm 19:14, "Let the words of my mouth and the meditation of my heart, be acceptable in Thy sight, O LORD, my strength and my Redeemer" (KJV).

Elvis spent considerable time with our church youth. Duane Knight recalls Elvis taking him and Ken Carter for a ride in his new Cadillac down Main Street in Memphis. After the initial shock of his stardom, we were glad for his success, yet all of us were concerned about his spiritual condition.

Maybe you've heard that Elvis was kicked out of First Assembly of God in Memphis. Or there was another false rumor that he tried out unsuccessfully for the Blackwood Brothers Quartet. Now the truth is, some young men formed a group called "The Songfellows." They were having tryouts for an opening. Elvis was very interested, but some dissuaded him, as they knew his style and wiggle wouldn't fit. Jimmy Hamill, the pastor's son, and Cecil Blackwood often joked about not letting the superstar Elvis be part of their quartet.

Elvis deeply influenced many people he was close to. It's true, he gave new Cadillacs to people he walked past in a dealership. He was generous to lots of folks. But as his personal life began to degenerate, he pulled numerous ones down with him. There was lots of gold and glitz, fame, fortune, bright lights, Hollywood, mansions, a fleet of luxury cars, two jet aircrafts and millions of admirers. He became a prisoner of his own success.

Elvis's behavior became more irrational. Once when he became irritated at a TV show, he took his revolver and shot out the television set in his hotel room. Around his neck he not only wore a cross, but a Buddha and the Star of David. He reportedly told a friend, "I just don't want to make a mistake." So he trusted in all three.

Terry Blackwood really wanted to help Elvis and have a ministry in Vegas, but Terry told me, "Gene, I tried to lift people up and influence them toward God. But as time went along, I found that instead of me lifting them up, they were dragging me down. So that's why I left and came back home to Memphis."

Not long after Elvis's death from a drug overdose, I happened to meet with J. D. Sumner in a Nashville cafe on "Music Row." J. D. was always a special friend to me. When we'd talk on the phone, his voice was like a deep, friendly bass growl. J. D. had big diamonds on several fingers. He proudly explained that these costly treasures were gifts from Elvis. Each marked a special success in their mutual careers together.

I don't want to elaborate, but Elvis's influence on some of his associates was not positive. One fellow entertainer once compared Elvis to Jesus. Such was the spell he seemed to cast on those who were close to him.

Today, anytime we have out-of-town guests, there's one place they want to see—Graceland. It doesn't matter whether it's day or night, raining or snowing; the crowds are always there. I've talked with people from Europe, Asia, Africa and Australia. The main reason they've come to Memphis is to see where Elvis lived, settled, and where he died and is buried. We've traveled to over 130 countries around the world. Whenever I tell people I'm from Memphis, they exclaim, "Elvis Presley!" Then they ask, "Did you ever see him or speak to him?" When I share some stories of our youth together, they act like I'm some kind of a god. I've even been in remote areas that have never heard of Jesus, but shockingly, they have heard of Elvis!

Recounting the story puts an ache in my heart. Millions have acclaimed him as a great success. Yet I think of our times in church, the purity of his courtship with my friend Dixie, and the stardom, loose living, divorce, loneliness, and the drugs and more drugs.

What might have happened if his God-given talent had been used for God? How might he have influenced many for Christ? No one can truly judge another one's eternal welfare, but Jesus in Scripture warns, "What is a man advantaged if he gains the whole world and lose himself, or be cast away?" (Luke 9:25,KJV).

11

JUST PASTOR THAT SUNDAY SCHOOL CLASS

For some years, I had debated about God's will in my life. Helpful friends knew I was called to the ministry because of my deep dedication to the Lord. They knew it, but I didn't! There is a big difference between being a full-time Christian and being a full-time minister of the Gospel.

While still studying pharmacy, I shared my dilemma with a very caring friend, Cam Wilson. Cam Wilson was the minister of education at my home church. He helped me discover God's will. It happened like this.

When I went to Cam, he told me of a junior boys' Sunday school class. They had run off the last three teachers. They were rowdy and shall we say "not hungry for the Word!"

"Why don't you take that class of boys and be their pastor?" he challenged. "They've had teachers, but they need a pastor." Then he explained, "You must be thoroughly prepared or they'll take advantage of you. But the most important thing is what happens outside of class." He continued, "Why don't you get to know the boys personally. Visit them in their homes, take them on outings, call them during the week, and believe God that each of them will be saved before they leave your class."

The staff members that served my home church had a deep impact on my life. Youth pastors often seem to have deeper influence on young people than even the senior pastor. Maybe they are more approachable, available and more involved in our lives. Pastor Hamill wisely brought gifted men to our staff. Dave Scott, Ernie Wood, Warren Grant, and Forrest Arnold and their companions modeled the Christian life. These names are fresh in my mind forty years later. No, I don't remember a single sermon they preached, but I remember their love and caring attitude. I guess that's where real ministry begins.

Well, I not only found out a lot about my class that made my teaching more effective, I found out a lot about me! From that time I began to think seriously about full-time ministry.

My Sunday school teachers shaped my earliest concepts of ministry. Every Saturday night Sister Geneva Bassi, my teacher, would phone me. Being only age six, I felt so important! She'd always ask, "Gene, will you be in Sunday school tomorrow?" Well, church was never an option in our home. While some may debate on a weekly basis about church attendance, there was never any doubt where the Burgess family would be. For every birthday, Mrs. Bassi would send a nice card with five sticks of chewing gum taped inside. Special memories like these have stuck with me for over 50 years!

As a teenager, I was enthralled as Emmett Maum wove sports stories into our class time. Emmett, you see, was a sports writer for the Memphis Commercial Appeal, and he knew many of my heroes.

Some teachers may simply read a lesson to their class and walk away. But I'm proud of that vast army of people who are not simply teachers, but ministers. Their love, concern, and care for their class goes on all week long. Great will be their reward.

12

MAY DAY AND THE SCARLET CORD

You may wonder what a commercial aircraft's distress call has to do with a scarlet cord. Mrs. Hugh Barron would frequently ask prayer for her family and add, "I've put out the scarlet cord just like Rahab did in the Bible."

From my early Sunday school days I recalled the story of Rahab. She lived in the city of Jerico. Joshua sent out spies to scout the city's defenses. The spies were almost caught, but Rahab hid them. As a favor, she requested that when the Israelites came to conquer Jerico, they would spare her entire household. In order that the army would know which house to spare, she hung a scarlet cord out the window. When the city was destroyed, Rahab and all in her household were safe because of the scarlet cord.

The May Day distress call was the final message from the American Airline flight 476 headed for Chicago. The engine caught fire, which enveloped the wing. At the controls was a seasoned veteran of 15 years, Captain Hugh Barron. The gallant crew nursed the plane to within sight of the runway. Then the wing fell off. Everyone was killed instantly.

The next morning, the story of the plane crash was splashed across the front page of the newspaper. As I glanced at the photo, for some reason I read through the list of crew members. The captain's name, Hugh Barron, leaped out at me. Shocked, I thought of the prayers of his wife, Margaret Barron.

I could still hear Mrs. Barron requesting prayer for her husband. She often stated, "My husband, Hugh, is a good man and a good father and husband. He just doesn't feel he needs the Lord. But as Rahab put out the scarlet cord for her family, I'm trusting all of our household will be saved." Once she stated, "I've prayed for my husband for 20 years. I have the assurance God is going to save him."

But now her husband was dead. I wondered how the family could go on. How could they survive if their prayers were unanswered? But perhaps their prayers had been answered after all. I desperately hoped so.

I was so deeply concerned, because Don and Billy Barron were two of my closest boyhood friends. I had always envied them because their father loved them enough to buy them motorcycles. One had a bright red Harley, and the other had a blue one. Of course, they were only work bikes, since they had paper routes. My own dad did his best to keep me away from their escapades.

All four of the Barron kids earned their pilot licenses early in life. Hugh, Don, Billy and their sister Maggie were an adventurous lot. Guess they got it from their dad. Don recalls going to church on Sunday morning, and then in the afternoon flying with his dad in an air show. Mr. Barron was a stunt pilot in a "flying circus." Once he intentionally stalled the plane engine in mid-air, stepped out of the cockpit onto a tire and spun the propeller to restart the engine. This is what he did for "fun."

So you see how the kids inherited their adventurous spirit. Once I remember Billy flying down East Parkway at 100 miles an hour on his motorbike. Clinging with all my might, I was petrified. That's one reason I forbade my kids to ride motorcycles. But I never told them the crazy things I'd done.

Billy and Don had an especially deep walk with the Lord. Both felt called into the ministry. Periodically I joined them as they conducted special meetings. Their mom, affectionately called Sister Barron, was a saint. She was such a loving, caring person. Her prayers were essential as Don, age 18, and Billy, age 16, pioneered the Frayser Assembly of God in 1956.

Many Saturday nights I went home with them. Billy and I would sweep up the cigar butts at the rented VFW hall so the church could meet on Sunday. This family received little encouragement from the other four Assembly of God churches in Memphis.

Since Billy was my age, we spent more time together. Don was two years older. In our rec room on Beasley St., we'd often play ping-pong until late into the night.

Billy tended to be somewhat of a braggert at times. So periodically the youth at our church would try to "whittle him down" a bit. Once as part of a Youth For Christ quiz team, we all went to Bristol, Tennessee. Billy was truly a fabulous trumpet player. And he enjoyed showing off for the girls. Since my skills were limited, I decided to sabotage his performance. He strutted to the stage. With a flair, he put the trumpet to his lips and blew. His face turned red. He tried a second time. I was afraid he'd blow his brains out trying to get some sound out of the trumpet. Then the ping-pong ball shot out into the crowd. The place rocked with laughter. But Billy didn't think it was funny. That's when I disappeared for the rest of the day.

As the years rolled by, the church in Frayser flourished. Hundreds of lives were touched by its ministry. On the church's fifth anniversary, T.F. Zimmerman, the General Superintendent of the Assemblies of God spoke. "Don isn't old enough to be ordained," he said, "but he has already been pastoring for five years!"

For years Don felt his ministry should be linked with flying. Then a door opened for him to fly for Trans World Airlines (TWA). His brother, Billy, became the pilot and organist for evangelist Oral Roberts. Later he became one of the youngest pilots to fly for Delta Airlines. Their older brother, Hugh, flew for Frontier. Unfortunately, by this time their sister, Maggie, had passed away.

Again, I looked at the newspaper pictures of the crash. Tears streamed down my face as I read of Captain Barron's death. All these memories of my time with this special family flooded my mind. But my biggest concern was for Mr. Barron's spiritual condition. Apparently the family had prayed for him for 27 years with no results. I wept as I thought of him dying unprepared to meet the Lord.

About two weeks later, Billy came back to Memphis from their Tulsa home. I didn't want to bring up the topic of his dad's death, nor his spiritual condition. But Billy broached the subject himself, talking about how deep the pain of the loss was. And then the bombshell: "Gene, it would have been unbearable if my dad had not been saved!"

Billy continued, "You know my mom prayed faithfully for my dad 27 years. Two weeks before his death, he came in from a trip. The family was in the kitchen. You know my dad didn't talk a lot. But he thanked us for our prayers. Then he told us that the night before in his hotel room in Chicago, he gave his life to the Lord. Oh, how we all rejoiced."

This certainly was a boost to my faith. But Billy continued, "Rev. E.M. Clark, the Superintendent of the Illinois District, was on Dad's plane. Moments before take-off he received an emergency phone call. He left the plane just before the cabin door closed, and his life was spared. Dad was only ten seconds from touch down when the wing fell off. The control tower reported someone in the cockpit praying the Lord's Prayer."

One footnote to this story—on the morning of Captain Barron's death, Mrs. Barron was speaking to a ladies' group in Tulsa. At the last minute, she felt prompted to change her topic to "I Am The Resurrection!"

Years passed. We were overseas in missions most of the time. On our return to the USA, ministry invitations in the Dallas area allowed us to renew our friendship with Billy. He was now a captain with Delta and a music director at First Assembly, Dallas. Like a kid, he took me for a spin in both of his new cars: a Corvette and a Thunderbird. (Men are just little boys with more expensive toys.) That night Billy and his wife, Linda, Heather and I went to see the Dallas Cowboys play. That was the last time I saw my buddy.

Two years passed, and we were directing the Vine Servicemen's Center in UTAPAO, Thailand. My mom sent me a letter and newspaper clipping. It was Billy's obituary. Unknown to most people, he had been having some heart problems. He was jogging with a friend in Dallas on the day that he died. The doctor said his heart literally burst. He was 34 years old.

Heart problems ran in the Barron family. A heart attack eventually claimed Mom Barron. And Don was not exempt. Don was a captain for TWA (now American Airlines). He'd gradually moved up to pilot their largest aircraft, the Boeing 747 jumbo jet. He flew mostly to Europe and the Middle East. His wife, Lorraine, often went along when their family was grown.

In the prime of life, the grim reaper struck at Don. In 1979 he also had a heart attack, although over time he recovered. However, his flying career was apparently over.

Even though Don had been a pilot, he was never out of the ministry. After pioneering Frayser Assembly in Memphis, he went to Kansas City with the airline and pioneered a church there. Finally, when the family was stationed in Atlanta, he started two churches in that area.

Don also had a heart for missions. He wanted to find a way to raise more money for Speed-the-Light to buy missionary vehicles. He had been riding a bike increasingly longer distances to strengthen his heart. One day a unique idea came to him. *Why don't my son, Don Junior, and I pedal from Atlanta to Miami, Florida?* Together they set out on the adventure, stopping at churches along the way and getting sponsors to help with Speed-the-Light. The Lord kept them safe and helped them raise missionary funds. But most important of all, Don never had the slightest problem with his heart. He was completely healed!

Once they got to Miami, the men decided to continue on another 130 miles down to Key West. In all, Don and his son pedaled 923 miles and conducted services over a two-week period.

Now an unexpected twist. Along the way, several newspapers sent reporters to photograph and interview this father and son team. Providentially, Don kept the clippings.

In Miami, they went to see a caring doctor who had helped pilots regain their flying licenses. Don simply showed him the clippings of their 923-mile odyssey.

When the FAA examiners saw the evidence of his recovery, they made a rare concession—Don Barron would again fly the jumbo jets for TWA!

Now years have passed. Don reached the mandatory retirement age of 60. He's still active in ministry. In fact, at this writing he travels with several cruise lines serving as their onboard chaplain. Yes, his life also has been "sponsored by the Holy Spirit."

13

NEAR STAMPEDE AT MY FIRST REVIVAL

For many months I debated if God was calling me into full-time ministry. From being a youth leader of about 100 church teenagers, doors to preach began to open.

My first big opportunity came through a gracious old-time pastor, Brother Earl Adcock, who ministered faithfully and pioneered churches. He came to Memphis to begin Rugby Park, the third Assemblies of God church in Memphis. The pastor of my home church felt, however, that our city needed just one Assemblies of God church, the one he pastored.

I was excited. My very first revival, and they even printed posters with my picture! As a formality, I asked to put the poster on First Assembly's church bulletin board. No doubt I was foolish to think that my home church would support me, or members might even visit me one night at the revival when they were not having services. But the pastor would not allow it to be put on the board, so most of the members didn't even know I was preaching at Rugby Park.

Mom and Dad came to the opening service. I had never preached to my parents. They had preached to me many times. I was an average, playful, mischievous boy whom they knew, warts and all. Now I was supposed to tell them how to live the Christian life! As I sat on the platform, a kind of embarrassment came over me. I wished that either I wasn't there or they weren't there.

Each day I attended classes at the University of Tennessee College of Pharmacy. At night the services went reasonably well. As the last evening approached, I really wanted to impress the congregation. Maybe that's how the problem began, my trying to impress people. Boldly, I announced the grand finale, entitled "The End Time Drama." I'd heard Pastor Hamill repeat this sermon on Bible prophecy several times. Now, I'm still not an expert on Bible prophecy, but

40 years ago I knew even less. My notes were pretty well organized, and I could rely on them if necessary. So I approached the subject rather confidently.

Not far into the sermon, however, things kind of got crazy. That day I'd just gotten new glasses. Bad eyesight has plagued me since birth. My left eye is legally blind, and my right eye is correctable to about 20/40. My glasses have to be cut perfectly, or I'm in trouble. On the night of the grand finale, I discovered that my notes looked blurry with my new glasses. Oh well, not to worry. The message began with the signs of the Last Days and was to include in order: the Rapture of the Believers, Judgment Seat, Marriage Supper of the Lamb, the Great Tribulation, the Second Coming, the Great White Throne Judgment, etc.

Now I look back on the subject that evening and wonder how deranged I was to tackle such a huge subject. Anyhow, the night was hot, and the building was crowded as I strolled confidently to the pulpit. We got the Signs of the Times pretty well figured out as I was preaching. But somewhere between the Rapture and the Great White Throne Judgment, I got totally confused and disorganized. Since all good preachers speak for at least 30 minutes, I plunged onward past the ten-minute mark hoping that I would soon figure out what I was supposed to be saying.

The longer I preached, the more confused I got. Sheer terror gripped my heart. Things got worse; people started leaving as I tried to find the caboose. More and more people left. Finally, it was over! I thought to myself, *There's no way I can ever preach again. And who would want me to preach anyhow?*

Pastor Adcock, always an encourager, shook my hand declaring, "That was quite a sermon young man!"

Yeah, I thought, *one I'll never forget.* Then I expressed regret for making such a mess of the closing night's meeting and making countless doctrinal errors. I apologized that so many had left the service.

The pastor looked amazed and asked, "Don't you know where they went?" No, I assumed home or to the nearby restaurant. "Follow me." He led me from the sanctuary. Just down the hall we entered a prayer room jammed with people seeking God.

The pastor explained, "As you were preaching, the Holy Spirit touched people, and one by one they came here to repent and to seek the Lord."

At that moment, I did not know whether to laugh or cry. I guess I had scared them half to death. I really don't know what I said. But the bottom line was, if God could use a confused message delivered by a blurry-eyed, terrified young man, surely He was a miracle-working God. Never have I doubted God's call since then. And never again have I attempted an entire message like that either!

14

I COULDN'T LET HER GET AWAY

I had to find out her name, find out something about her. Never had I spoken to a group where one person, especially a young lady, had caught my attention.

The lighting in the sanctuary wasn't very bright, and with my borderline vision, I would have missed her if she weren't sitting near the front. (Girls, if you want to snare a young, single preacher, sit down front!)

My being in Toronto's Danforth Gospel Temple (Canada) was an accident, it appeared. The plans originally called for me to speak in a large downtown church, Evangel Temple. But a prospective pastor was scheduled to candidate that day. Dr. Harry Faught graciously accepted this young lay preacher at the last minute.

Ministry in Toronto, Canada was my first stop. Ahead was a three-month odyssey that would take me across much of Europe and the Middle East. Later, I discovered that this was truly sponsored by the Holy Spirit.

My dad had offered me a ten-day trip to London, England as a graduation present after UT College of Pharmacy. His businesses were doing well, and I think that he sensed God had other plans for me besides pharmacy. Being from a strong missions church, I longed to visit missionaries and see what their ministries were like. I also sensed, (I'd now been preaching a bit for three or four years) that I might minister along the way.

Two men took special interest in me. For reasons I've never understood, they stuck their necks out for me—a relatively inexperienced lay preacher. I've deeply admired these two men for 40 years, long after their recommendation.

Willard Cantelon was a tall, imposing, brilliant man. He could quote Scriptures by the chapters. His messages were captivating. He'd preach for an hour without any notes. He encouraged people to bring guests to his revival meetings. Then he would paint lovely oils in only 10 or 15 minutes and present the painting to the one bringing the most visitors. Many people came to Jesus through his ministry. He wrote letters of recommendation for me to some of the key pastors of the largest churches in Europe, as well as several missionaries.

The other man, Dr. J. Philip Hogan, was the director of our Division of Foreign Missions of the Assemblies of God for many years. He was deeply admired and respected by many mission organizations. Dr. Hogan was a powerful man, a gifted leader, and an organizer. You never doubted what was on his mind. Again, for some reason, he also made contacts for me in Europe and the Middle East.

With men like Cantelon and Hogan in my corner, the doors opened. I think how fortunate I was to have such help. Countless other good men often have no one to take an interest in them. Maybe this is one reason I've sought to reach out to younger ministers and those who have gone through painful struggles with no one to help them.

I got to minister in Toronto, Canada, through their contacts. That night, I met Heather Reed! She was a 21-year-old college student at The University of Toronto and a deeply devoted Christian. The lady she sat with was her mother. I had to act fast before the crowd left after service. No, I don't remember what I preached!

So I asked Heather's mom, "Where do the young people go after church?"

Well, there weren't many young people present that night, but Mrs. Reed asked, "Would you like to come to our house for a snack?"

Heather seemed fascinated that I was not only a new pharmacist, but I also had a teaching position at the University. Organic chemistry was my specialty and her worst nightmare. She thought I was a genius.

The next day, Heather's brother, Bryan, took me around Toronto. Then we went back to the Reeds' for supper. Her dad was a very committed Christian. He also was a gifted architect, specializing in schools and churches. You can be sure I got Heather's address. This began a three-year mailbox romance.

After only one year in pharmacy, I burned the bridge behind me and launched out by faith into a traveling evangelistic ministry. Yes, I had a special "burden" for Toronto. If I were within 500 miles I would just "drop by." As time went along, there was an increasing "leading" to conduct more meetings in New York, Michigan, New England and of course Ontario, Canada.

After two years in this relationship I decided it was time to get married. But there was a problem. Heather still had one year left to finish her B.A. degree. She couldn't hope to finish her education with being married and on the road 50 weeks a year. I selfishly wanted her to postpone her education and get married.

Being a proper southern gentleman, I asked her father for his daughter's hand. Frank Reed was a fine, outstanding Christian businessman. In fact, the Reeds mirrored the values of my own family exactly. When the church doors were opened, they were there. They helped and took part in every way possible. They lived the gospel 24/7.

Anyhow, Dad Reed reminded me of his financial investment in Heather's education. But wisely, he didn't put his foot down. He wanted me to decide. Heather was glad I had finally popped the question, but more than a little annoyed that I, being a rather wise young man, wanted her to quit school. Yes, my heart was ruling my head I must admit.

In the emotion of the moment, I wondered how much it would help for a preacher's wife to have a B.A. degree in Home Economics (which I playfully called "Can Opening 101"). And besides, for the next year, I couldn't even see her one time as my meetings were already scheduled for Southern California and the Deep South.

Well, one of my sayings, "Preachers are borderline human," was true. This would have been a very unwise decision for her to quit school. Her degree gave her a foundation to later complete her Master's degree, and to teach in high school. But it was a very lonely year.

Several dear friends like Gene and Ruth Martin encouraged me not to get married for several years. Their concern was I would lose my appeal to teens and young people. Well, I'll admit, when church services were over and I was traveling on the road, I hung out a lot with the young people. Being with these groups helped dispel the loneliness.

To some, having a fine car and traveling the country may have seemed glamorous. But believe me that gets old in a few months. In fact, even after we were married we were not in one city for more than two weeks for almost six years. It was often lonely.

Finally, the wedding day approached. My Aunt Nell was excited. She had been there the night the Holy Spirit flowed through my life at youth camp. She made Heather's going away outfit, a beautiful white silk suit. When she asked the cost of mailing it from Memphis to Toronto, the cost surprised her. In her typical fashion she declared, "I'll just take it myself!" And she along with Ma Scott, and Homer and Donna Hamby drove over 1100 miles to our wedding in Toronto.

Homer Hamby had been a close Christian friend who was a year ahead of me at UT Pharmacy School. In fact, he had a dorm room at school while I had to ride the bus for an hour each day. So living at some distance from the school, I often borrowed his bed between classes.

Men, I found out, are the most unwelcome people as a wedding draws close. In fact, my input on the ceremony wasn't welcome at all. All I requested was that Ken Carter sing, "Whither Thou Goest I Will Go." In reality, we never dreamed where the next 40 years would take us.

At that time, Ken and Sherry Carter were living near Washington, D. C. Ken was a soloist for the United States Air Force Singing Sergeants. Later, we occasionally crossed paths with the Carters, since we both now traveled full-time. Ken had been a friend since childhood. When I first started preaching, he often came and helped by singing. He still has a tremendous booming, bass-baritone voice. I remember that while with The Singing Sergeants, he helped me in a crusade in Pennsylvania one night. The next day, President John F. Kennedy was assassinated. I still recall walking down the hall to my hotel room, when a sobbing woman opened the door and screamed the news of his death. Ken invited me to D. C. for a special memorial service for the slain President. He sang at this most traumatic time in our nation's history. I was honored he would also sing at our wedding.

Dr. Faught did a flawless job at the wedding ceremony. Maybe I should mention that since I was an evangelist, I had no idea how to properly compensate him for his services. I asked him, "Dr. Faught, what is a proper amount to give as an offering for your ministry at the wedding?"

He replied that I should simply give as much as I thought it was worth. Well, that really perplexed me. Thinking how much I loved Heather, I thought I should give him at least $100. This $100 in 1965 would probably be equivalent to almost $1,000 today. Many pastors would still be pleased with just $100.

As I stood on the platform, I recalled standing on that same platform when I first saw Heather three years earlier. I realized all that I had received and how God had helped me. But this time, being on the platform was far more frightening than standing there preaching. In fact, as I was about to put the ring on Heather's finger, I dropped it. The ring rolled across the floor and into a vent. Dr. Faught wisely motioned to fake it, so I acted as if I was placing the ring on her finger. After the ceremony, a little boy reached in and retrieved the wedding ring, and I finally put it on Heather's finger.

The Canadian custom was to have a sit-down dinner for the wedding guests. When the meal was over that day, I had the uneasy sense that something was about to happen. As we gathered around the lily pond for photos, I saw my brothers, Ron and Phil, eyeing Heather's cousin Bob Smith. Then I noticed them whispering to Homer Hamby, my best man. The next thing I knew, the three of them had Bob Smith and were throwing him, tuxedo and all, into the lily pond.

Most of the locals were thrilled to see Bob getting paid back for all the people he had tormented over the years. Fearing the party might get rough, Heather and I quickly left for our honeymoon.

Our honeymoon carried us to Montreal, to Quebec City and on to New York City. From there we traveled to our first revival meeting in Knoxville, Tennessee with Pastor and Mrs. J. L. Schaffer. This was a scary experience for Heather, to suddenly be a preacher's wife and be expected to know all about the ministry. Mrs. Schaffer (Blythe) gave her lots of encouragement and support.

Heather developed a talent for using puppets, which she used to teach children in family crusades while I preached to the adults. She also played the piano. Whatever I may have accomplished in life and ministry, much is due to her.

15

"WE DON'T WANT ANY OF YOUR MEDICINES!"

"We don't want any of your medicines." These seemed like harsh, unkind words from such a polite, soft-spoken medical doctor. Doctor Habib Iskander was the head of our Lillian Trasher Orphanage in Assiout, Egypt.

Lillian Trasher, a young New York nurse, began this orphanage while in her early twenties. She had turned down marriage with an outstanding doctor because she felt called as a missionary to Egypt. She invested nearly 60 years caring for literally hundreds of homeless boys, girls, and widows. Momma Thrasher went on to be with Jesus just weeks before I arrived at the desert outpost.

Her bedroom was mine during my time of ministry there. It was just as she left it. On the dresser were her comb, brush, Bible and a photo taken when she was a young lady. It was like a sacred sanctuary.

With nearly 800 children, the Assiout Orphanage functioned like a well-contained city. Older boys grew crops, milked cows and learned to make tables and beds. The girls and the widows sewed clothes for the infants and also for the staff. This was a unique faith experiment in that day. Today, the Assemblies of God sponsors many thousands of children all over the world like those in the Assiout Orphanage.

It was a joy to speak to the kids, play with them and just watch this well-oiled machine run so smoothly. My departure back to Cairo began just before sunup. Doctor Iskander took me to the train station. Scores of people were asleep on the train platform floor. We carefully stepped over them to board my train.

I was so deeply impressed by the orphanage and the wonderful work that they were doing, I wanted to have a part. So I told my new friend, Dr. Iskander, "I noted in your pharmacy many of your medicines were out of date, and the drugs aren't very effective anymore. The operating room seems ancient. Now that I have my Doctors Degree in Pharmacy, I have a lot of contacts. So when I get back to Memphis, I'll tell people about your need, and I'll be sending you some money and some medicines."

His response shook me! "Gene, we don't want any of your money or medicines. You can keep them!" I was stunned; surely they needed help. His kindness seemed to suddenly vanish. Then he asked, "Do you know what we really want? We want you to come back here and help us!"

Stunned, shocked, startled, and speechless, I barely choked out a goodbye. Tears flowed down my cheeks.

During the eight-hour desert trip back to Cairo, God spoke to me. As the wheels clicked against the rails, I kept hearing, "We want you to come back and help us."

Was it possible even as a young lay preacher who had a lot of ministry, I had tried to bribe God? Had I tried to bribe Him with tithes and missionary offerings, preaching and leading in ministries without pay? Was I afraid of total surrender? And if I did surrender, would God make me do something awful like being full-time in the ministry, or even worse, being a missionary?

Now, I'd come from one of the great missionary churches in America. The church had given literally millions of dollars to missions, yet relatively few of our young people had entered full-time Christian service. Like many of my peers, I'd march up to the altar each time we had a missionary speak. We'd all sing, "I'll go where you want me to go dear Lord." But now, was God speaking through someone in Egypt to tell me it was time to "put up or shut up?"

Another life-impacting thing happened on the journey. Earlier I mentioned a vision I had had at age 16 at youth camp. God's Spirit flowed into my life that night. I've never been the same since. Yes, you and I both need periodic updates of God's outpouring in our lives. But in that puzzling vision, I was speaking in tongues to Arabic or Middle Eastern people. Then it struck me—I had just been speaking in Egypt, Jordan, Lebanon, and Israel to the very same type of people I'd seen in my vision seven years before!

On my return to Memphis, I accepted a position at the University of Tennessee College of Pharmacy to teach laboratory classes. Also, I practiced pharmacy in a local store. Even though my profession gave me open doors of ministry, I could hardly wait for the weekends to come. Each weekend I would minister God's Word in a different church. Usually I would return to Memphis late Sunday night and be at the university early on Monday morning. This killing pace went on for nearly a year.

Besides teaching at the university, practicing pharmacy, and preaching on weekends, I also had a weekly inspirational TV program. Every Friday morning at 6:45 a.m., I hosted "Above The Clouds" on Channel 13 from the Peabody Hotel.

Now it makes me tired just thinking about all I was doing. Also, I organized a ministry for troubled youth. It was called Life Line, a part of Memphis Youth For Christ. Youth For Christ in those days was an effective, international, inter-denominational ministry mainly to teens.

Among those who assisted me on the Board of Directors were outstanding Christian business and professional men. Eddy McAteer, called the "Friend of Five Presidents," was a key part of this outreach. Also, Judge Bill Leffler and the Memphis Police Chief played vital roles.

So many came along side of me in these ministries that as the coordinator, I often got too much praise. The real work was done by a large, committed core of volunteers who reached out to those who had been in trouble with the law.

But I did preside over at least one giant fiasco. Memphis Juvenile Authorities talked with me about a summer camp. It would be a fun time for teenage boys who had been locked up for rather minor crimes.

A nice, secluded place was found for the camp. Gracious volunteers served as cooks and counselors for the 40 boys. There were some difficulties, but finally, as I awaited the last day of camp, it happened. One of the boys escaped.

Later, we found out he'd escaped even while in jail. Yet the authorities blamed me for allowing him to escape in an open-air camp. Anyhow, search parties combed the woods. Later, the sheriff caught him hitchhiking back to Memphis. This ministry can be exciting.

Eddie McAteer and I became very close friends during this time. He had certainly encouraged me in many ways. Through this work that Eddie and I did together with Youth For Christ, we met the founder and president, Doctor Kelly Bihl, who came to Memphis. Kelly was a great man of God who, like others, for some reason took time for me.

"Dr. Bihl," I said one day, "my dad is a full-time Christian and is constantly ministering to prisoners and filling in for pastors. So I wonder, how do you distinguish between being a 24/7 Christian and a 24/7 minister? In the New Testament," I said, "it seemed like everybody was in the ministry."

So Kelly began questioning me, asking, "What is it that you enjoy doing most? God put that desire there, if you're walking close to Him."

But I protested, "I don't feel like a preacher or a minister!" Sometimes finding God's will is like driving through the fog. When the fog is heavy, you go slowly; as it clears you can speed up. So for me, it was go slow for several months.

Finally it was time to make a contract with God. Here's the "deal" I made. "Dear Lord, if you want me in full-time gospel ministry, would you please do three things: one, provide places for me to preach; two, give me something worthwhile to say; and three, provide finances for me to get there."

The time came "to burn the bridge" of security. Leaving the university and my practice was tough in some ways. In those days, most of the ministers I knew were poor. Their cars were old, suits threadbare, and their homes clean but mediocre at best. Since I was no better than they, I was resigned to a lifetime of bare survival.

Over the years there have been times of financial stress, but time and again the Lord has come through. Yes, it's really true that He is able to do exceedingly abundantly more than we ask or think, (Ephesians 3:20). We have found God is faithful, and He has always kept His part of our bargain.

16

BURNING THE BRIDGE

From having a Doctor of Pharmacy degree with an assured future, to being a traveling evangelist waiting for the phone to ring, was a big change. There came a time I had to decide whether I was going to trust God for the rest of my life or trust my career. The future life I was looking toward seemed unpredictable. Many ministers in those days barely survived. I realized that I was no better than any of them.

The three-month ministry trip to Europe and the Middle East changed my life forever. The challenge of Dr. Habib Iskander in Assiout, Egypt haunted me, "We want you to come back here and help us!" Over the years, I've had wonderful fellowship with Habib and his wife Ruth. Sometimes we don't know how a few words directed by the Holy Spirit can change someone's life forever.

Upon graduation from the University of Tennessee and passing the State Board, I began to practice pharmacy and teach some at the university. Unfortunately, I got fired from my first pharmacy job. The owner of the store got angry because I would not work on Sunday. It was humbling to be fired from my first job. Soon, however, another pharmacy offered me a job at an even better salary.

Most of my time was spent at the university. Being in postgraduate work in pharmaceutical chemistry meant long hours of study, plus research. Our division had grants to modify the LSD molecule in hopes that it could be useful in medicine.

For some time I had been earnestly praying to know God's will for my life. Rebellion against God's plan wasn't the problem. But understanding God's will was. In the New Testament, it seemed everybody was in ministry. The line between clergy and laity was blurred. The dilemma: was I supposed to be a layman like my dad who operated four pharmacies, served as a deacon, and filled pulpits occasionally, or should I enter the ministry full-time?

For the next year I was on contract with the university. But as the time dragged on, God's will for my life became clearer. Not everyone understands why

I studied pharmacy and was teaching at the university. My pastor, whom I greatly respected, one day frankly stated, "It's a shame you've wasted all these years of your life in pharmacy. By now, you could have had your Divinity degree instead of your Pharmacy degree."

Was it really a waste? There were 100 students in each of the three classes I taught in laboratory science. These were young people who would never come to hear me preach. But many opportunities came to share my faith with them.

Dr. Seldon Feurt was the Dean of The College of Pharmacy. He was the inventor of the tranquilizer gun that is used to sedate animals. He was a brilliant man with a great heart. Dr. Feurt was a church leader who had never heard of being born again. Even though I was at the bottom of the staff totem pole, we developed an unusual friendship. He helped support the YFC camp I directed. Then when he came to hear me preach, Dr. Feurt accepted Jesus. Was it really a waste?

In my pre-pharmacy study at Evangel College, I was sheltered. What a blessing to have born-again, Spirit-filled professors with their PhD degrees teach you science from a biblical perspective.

But later, in the secular university, the professors boasted of their broad-mindedness and their weekend exploits. Profanity and off-colored jokes were routine. It helped me understand what our Christian young people endure when they go to a secular university. When I worked in the pharmacy, I also gained an insight into the business world. Often it was hurried and stressful. Periodically, I was cussed out because a prescription was too expensive or people had to wait too long. Now when people come to church after a very busy week and give their tithes, I know a bit about their lives. No, I believe God intentionally took me on a different route into the ministry and it was not a waste.

Another man of God gave wise counsel as I debated about God's will. Dr. J. Robert Ashcroft was a kind, brilliant and caring man. He was the president of Evangel, our liberal arts college, while I was a student there. He was also the father of Attorney General John Ashcroft.

Evangel, Dr. Ashcroft, and my family were closely linked. My dad, Doyle, served on the board of directors. He worked tirelessly promoting the college. Many young people have told me they stayed in Burgess Hall, the dorm named for my father. Periodically Dr. Ashcroft would visit our home. Even though he was a prominent person, he invested time in counseling me.

One of my many concerns was that I had no formal Bible school training. What practical good was a Doctor of Pharmacy degree in the ministry? I asked Dr. Ashcroft if I should go to Bible college. His reply amazed me. "Gene, many people go to Bible college and never put to use what they learn. But I believe you have a solid Christian foundation. So I recommend you take accredited Bible correspondence courses. Then be a Bible student the rest of your life."

I still have the little brochure Dr. Ashcroft helped me design. We joked together that if I did become an evangelist, I'd get more invitations if I'd shot a few people and been in jail.

When my contract at UT was finished, it was time to launch into full-time ministry, by "burning the bridge" of security. As I began to travel as an evangelist, something became clearer. Most other young evangelists first conducted revival meetings for friends they had made in Bible school. But I'm so grateful to pastors who believed in me. It's amazing, from the first step of faith, doors opened. Usually Heather and I were booked to preach 45 to 48 weeks a year.

Oh yes, there was one other part of the contract I'd made with God. All evangelists enjoy speaking in the large, thriving churches. This usually requires many years of experience and some kind of fantastic story of a former life of crime. I promised the Lord if I had the privilege of ministering in the largest churches, that I'd go to the smallest, struggling churches as well. During my eight years of full-time ministry as a traveling evangelist, we did minister in many of the largest churches in the USA and Canada. And overseas, we had the privilege of ministering in what is the largest church in the world with Pastor Yonggi Cho in Seoul, Korea. We responded to invitations from small, struggling churches as well, and God always supplied our needs.

In the first eight years of our ministry, we were never in one city more than two weeks. In fact, our wedding gifts were packed away for over ten years before we were able to open them up and enjoy them. Our lives in the ministry have truly been "sponsored by the Holy Spirit."

17

OUTSMARTED BY A CAT

✦

(Dedicated to Cat Lovers Everywhere!)

For two years, I traveled all over the country before Heather and I were married. It was lonely driving long distances, eating alone, staying alone, etc. To some it may have looked glamorous, but not in reality. Yet many inspiring, exciting and even crazy things happened during those days, such as the smart cat episode.

Many have asked how they can get into the ministry. The answer is easy: start where you are, use the talent you have, and start doing something to help people. It's good to start gradually. Oh yes, also stay out of debt!

For two years before I "burned the bridge," I ministered on weekends around the Mid-South. Valuable relationships were built with a number of pastors. When I went into full-time traveling evangelistic ministry, many of these men invited me for crusades.

Weekend ministry had been a growing time, and was exciting for me, especially times with Jimmy Blackwood when he was trying out his new souped-up convertible. His dad, James, was known worldwide as a great man and gospel singer. Jimmy desperately wanted to sing also. Yet, he was rather shy, and despite lessons from two different voice teachers, his singing talent had not yet fully developed.

James asked if I'd take Jimmy with me for weekend ministry trips. Jimmy played the piano and sang. Frankly, in those early days I was glad for his company, but I wasn't sure he'd make it singing. Well, that's just how little I knew. In the years that followed, Jimmy Blackwood led the Blackwood Brothers Quartet after his father retired, and he has become one of the most outstanding gospel-singing evangelists in our country today.

When I left pharmacy, God opened many doors for me. In fact, sometimes there was no time to rest after a tiring series of revival meetings. Birmingham,

Alabama was the site of a great spiritual outpouring. Pastor Selby McManus was a vital part of this genuine revival. My Uncle Ken Sparks was saved in that meeting. Once again, I gave all I had, preaching night by night, and closed the meetings totally drained and exhausted.

The following Monday, I faced the long drive from Birmingham to Los Angeles. Sitting on the edge of the motel bed, I thought ahead to all the hundreds of miles I would have to drive alone. Most of the drive would be on two-lane highways, since the interstate system was still being constructed.

My vision also was barely adequate. Already, I'd seen many horrible wrecks in the few months of traveling full-time. Passing long trailer trucks on crowded two-lane roads was especially scary, since I did not see that well. As I sat in the motel room, weakness overwhelmed me. I didn't have energy even to pack the car, much less drive 2,000 miles! After a temporary pity party, a small voice seemed to say, "You don't have to drive 2,000 miles today. Just get up and go as far as you can each day. You don't have to be in L. A. for a week." Some smart person said that anxiety grows when we try to fight tomorrow's problems with today's energy. At that low point of energy and drive, the Lord reminded me of this. Sure enough, I got to the West Coast safely and enjoyed a full three months of successful meetings as planned.

Oh, I almost forgot about the smart cat. Some of my dear friends have doubted a few of the stories that I have told, and in fact, they even accuse me of making them up. Sometimes calloused individuals refer to our feline friends as "dumb animals." But many have proved, as in this case, that they are smarter than a lot of people. Cross my heart, this actually happened.

The city was Tulsa, Oklahoma. The revival crusade was with Pastor Don Mallough. He and his wife, Darlene, were some of the greatest evangelists of that day, before they became pastors of the church in Tulsa. A kind, middle-aged couple provided my lodging.

When I arrived at their home, the couple offered to help unload the car. I noticed a rather mangy cat by the door. As I was getting settled, I flinched—the cat was up on the table. The couple made no move to evict the cat. Instead, they began to feed him. This cat could really eat. Never had I seen such a bold cat, and one with such a huge appetite.

During the week of meetings, the cat ruled the house. Several times I wanted to tell my host to please get the cat off the countertops and the kitchen table. But since I was only a guest, I thought it was well to keep my mouth shut. The cat really ruined my visit. He didn't smell very good either.

When it was time to leave, I was relieved to get away from that horrible cat. Finally, the car was packed and I started the engine. Then the door of the home burst open. "Wait," my host shouted, "you forgot your cat!"

"I don't have a cat!" I replied, amazed. "Isn't that cat in the house your cat?"

"No!" he shot back! Then I wondered, whose cat was it after all?

At that moment we realized what must have happened. This was a stray cat, smart enough to see a good thing. My host was afraid of offending me by complaining about the cat. I was afraid of offending my host by bringing up the subject of what I thought was his cat. Thus, both of us gritted our teeth for an entire week because we did not face this problem cat.

Is there a lesson here? I think so; it's all about communication. Because we were afraid to clearly communicate what was a concern to us, we were both frustrated to the point of exasperation, and nothing got settled. So I guess it's better, if we have a true concern or problem, to talk about what annoys us in the right way. This will spare us a great deal of frustration. And you can see, sometimes cats are smarter than people!

18

CONFUSION IN THE HOSPITAL

The rain and the sleet pounded the car the whole two-hour trip. "Please Lord, don't let this be the night the baby comes," I prayed. Reaching my folks' home at 743 Beasley in Memphis, I was so exhausted I could hardly walk. I literally stumbled into the house. The door hit something—a packed suitcase!

Momentary insanity overwhelmed me. Maybe she could drive herself to the hospital and just phone me how it went! Just kidding! Well, you know having a baby is tough on husbands too!

Heather was having painful contractions as we sped to the downtown Baptist Hospital. She was admitted immediately. It was customary for prospective dads to pace the halls. But I was so weary, I just sat down and immediately fell into a deep sleep. The next thing I knew, the doctor was beside me with the happy news. It was a healthy baby girl, and Heather was doing great! Deborah Michelle joined us on December 29, 1969.

Unfortunately, there was some confusion in the hospital nursery. At the viewing time, I arrived with my camera. As the nurse showed the baby, I shot almost a whole roll of film, and was amazed at what a fine offspring we had produced. Then someone commented, "That's a fine boy you've got there!"

"No," I explained, "it's a girl."

"Funny," the other dad commented, "usually they don't put blue booties on little girls."

Had there been some mix-up in the nursery? Then a prissy nurse closed the curtains for the nursery viewing. Boy was I shook! I pounded on the door and demanded, "Do I have a boy or a girl? Did you get the wrong booties on the baby? Did you show me the wrong baby?" Well, the latter was true. I had taken almost a whole roll of film of the wrong baby.

Now, a minor problem at home: my dad just knew we'd have a boy. The Burgess dynasty was at stake. He was sure the babies got switched in the nursery. It seems funny now, but for several days he didn't accept the fact that Debbie was ours.

Soon, I had to leave for meetings in Kansas. At ten days old, Debbie had her first airplane ride when Heather joined me there. Since our hotel did not have a crib, it seemed fitting that we bed her down in a dresser drawer. Colic and stomach pains plagued Deborah constantly. On some long drives, it seemed she never stopped crying. It was hard on all of us, but Heather was an ideal, loving, and caring mom.

Deborah never met a stranger. Wherever we went, people loved her. Often, a family would say, "I wish you'd let us take her home!" And because the hotel rooms were often too small for the three of us, we sometimes responded, "Here, bring her back tomorrow night!"

Som's entry into the world was much more dramatic. It was 1973 at UTAPAO Air Force Base in Thailand. The Holy Spirit had definitely led us there after we had filled in for a missionary in Bangkok. The Vietnam War was in full swing, and 10,000 troops were stationed at UTAPAO. Vietnam was only a short hop away for the 8-engine B52 bombers and KC135 aerial tankers. But we were missionaries, and the Air Force did not deliver civilian babies. And we were about to have our second.

Three-and-a-half hours away in Bangkok, the Seventh Day Adventist hospital was the best alternative. Our Canadian missionary friends, Carl and Dorothy Young, invited Heather to stay with them in their Bangkok home. But Som decided he didn't want to face the new world on the projected date. When he was a week overdue, Heather felt she was taxing the Youngs' hospitality. So she finally went to the hospital to have labor induced. We paid extra to get an English-speaking doctor. The nurses spoke only Thai, and our Thai was extremely limited.

After the contractions started, they ran out of oral medicine, and finally hooked Heather up to an IV. This whole time I was being a good husband, not going to sleep and staying by her side to help. Being a pharmacist, I checked the IV. It was labeled "Glucose." Even a layman knows glucose does not induce labor. I went down the halls hollering in English for the nurses to come and fix the IV. They tried to calm me down, which only made me more excited. Finally, the doctor came and ordered me to leave.

The hospital had only one air-conditioned room. With the sweltering, tropical temperature, we paid extra dollars for this also. Now here I was—expelled from the delivery room. I was sitting in a rather uncomfortable chair, waiting and waiting and waiting. "Why," I asked myself, "should I sit in this uncomfortable chair for hours, when the bed in the maternity ward lies empty?" It doesn't take a rocket scientist to size this up.

So I slipped off my shirt and shoes, and relaxed a little while on Heather's bed. The next thing I knew, someone burst into the room, flipped on the lights and screamed something in Thai. Again, I had drifted into a deep sleep, I'm sorry to admit. Blurry-eyed, the next thing I saw was them wheeling Heather and little Som into the room.

We were excited about having a baby boy. Soon I dismissed myself, went to the jewelry store and bought Heather a lovely ruby ring. She has worn that ring often, and we're grateful to God for the safe delivery of our fine baby boy.

When I went to register his name, Philip Eugene, I guess the pen "slipped" and out came the name Doyle Eugene Burgess III. Heather thought I was kidding until she saw Som's birth certificate. Som joined our team on March 1,1973.

So now we had a problem—my dad was living, and went by the name Doyle. I didn't like Eugene—my teachers called me this when I got into trouble. As a temporary compromise we called him Som, the Thai word for "Third" from the name, Doyle Eugene Burgess III.

All through school and college he was called Som. When he entered the work force as a computer programmer, he chose the name Doyle. But the name Som has stuck among our family and close friends.

And despite his father messing up his most precious possession—his name—he's done exceedingly well in life.

19

LOST IN A CANADIAN BLIZZARD

In 1970 we made a very eventful six-month venture all across western Canada in the winter. Now you want to know why smart evangelists head south for the winter, and we headed north? Pastors had told me, "If you come up here in the summer, everybody will be in the fields, or boating at the lake. But they'll come to church in zero-degree weather, just so the snow isn't blowing." Well, for the entire winter, the attendance and response in these churches was tremendous!

For six months, we drove thousands of miles across the Canadian prairies. Our services started in Winnipeg, Manitoba. These folks claim that Winnipeg, not Chicago, is the windiest city in North America. It was October, and the snow was already falling.

One of the great churches of Canada was the historic downtown Calvary Temple. Pastor H. H. Barber was internationally known as a leader and preacher. My youthful enthusiasm kept me from being too awed to fill that pulpit.

Part of my "bargain with God" was if He'd open the doors of some of our largest churches, I'd gladly accept ministry in the most struggling home mission churches. So during these months in Canada, we ministered in not only the largest churches, but in young, small, struggling churches as well.

Our church revival meetings were interspersed with Youth for Christ rallies. In those days, YFC had a great impact on the prairie cities and towns. We spoke to large crowds in city auditoriums in Calgary, Alberta and in tiny schoolhouses in places like Esterhazey, Saskatchewan. Once, after service, we stayed in a rural farm home. The overnight snowfall was so great, horses had to pull us out to the nearest road the next morning.

Billy Graham has written of his adventures traveling with Canadian Youth For Christ in the prairies. Night after night, he preached and drove long distances for the next night's meeting. Well, I was no Billy Graham, but this was exactly what we experienced.

One night we were scheduled for a rally 90 miles north of Regina, Saskatchewan. The next night, we had to be in Calgary, Alberta by 5 p.m. The distance was 600 miles. So after the Friday night meetings in a small city, we decided to drive the 90 miles onward to Regina to spend the night. Of course, it was snowing and rather treacherous to drive. As we gassed up, a man pulled up beside us and asked where we were headed. When we said Regina, he exclaimed, "Me too! Why don't you follow me? I know a short cut that's not on the map that will get us there a lot quicker."

Soon, we were on our way out into a wilderness. Suddenly, on this lonely prairie road, the man stopped and blocked the road. He got out of his car. The moonlight caught the silhouette of a rifle as he hurried toward us. We were sure he planned to shoot and rob us. There was no way to escape. All we could do was pray.

"Did you see that deer?" he shouted, coming to our window. We almost collapsed in relief. Someone said, "In the ministry, you must always be ready to preach, pray, or die." Well, we did certainly pray.

The next day, we would again see the mercy of the Lord. Regina to Calgary was roughly over 500 barren miles, with hardly a town or even a tree along the way, only miles of flat wheat land. Since there were few towns, and fewer hospitals along the Trans Canada Highway, special signs had been placed at intervals. These signs read "First Aid Station Ahead." No doctors were present, but local farmers had been trained in first aid. We came very close to needing them, or possibly a morgue that day. We had to arrive in Calgary by 5 p.m. Light snow was falling, but it wasn't slick. When it's about zero degrees, the snow on the road is firmly packed, and you can drive rather fast. Stopping is the problem!

I was driving about 70 miles per hour. It was almost a whiteout because of fog and snow. Out of the corner of my eye, I saw movement up ahead. Since we were in the middle of nowhere, I figured we were approaching something unusual. So I tapped the brakes lightly. Though we did slide some, we started to slow down. As the fog cleared we could see a man on the roadside waving a blanket to flag us down. A few yards further we came upon a horrible wreck. A cattle truck had crashed head-on into a Greyhound bus. If that man, or angel, hadn't been there waving that blanket, we would have plowed directly into the wreck. All of us would have been killed. Again, we realized this trip was truly "sponsored by the Holy Spirit."

Afterward, I thought of that flagman on the roadside. He reminded me of the need for believers to stand by life's highway and warn men to come to Jesus. Destruction could be just ahead.

Sometimes people ask, "What is the most unique experience you've had?" I've thought of the floating market place in Bangkok, Thailand or seeing the giraffes in Kenya's wildlife preserve. But these six months in Western Canada were some of the most memorable.

On one of our first days in Western Canada, I went out to start the car. It barely groaned. When I told the local pastor, he inquired, "You do have a block heater, don't you?" I thought he was talking about a hat for my head.

He asked if I hadn't seen cords sticking out of the grills of other cars. Then he explained, "In sub-zero temperature, the oil freezes, but a heating coil in the engine block plugged into an electric outlet keeps the oil flowing."

Now I did have plenty of anti-freeze in the car, but the engine was frozen like a block of ice. The only way to start the car was to get it either pushed or pulled up to 35 miles an hour. The only person willing to help pull me, drove a gasoline truck. Can you imagine being chained to a gasoline truck on a snowy road, trying to get your car up to 35 miles an hour? Yes, I did pray.

At the end of the first three months, we were in another of Canada's finest churches. It was Edmonton, Alberta's Central Pentecostal Tabernacle, pastored by Bob Taitenger. In those days, a church averaging over 1000 was unusual. This church had a four-year Bible college and influenced the entire region for God.

From Edmonton, we faced a 2,000-mile drive for three months of crusades down in sunny Southern California. But one by one those meetings got cancelled, mainly due to pastoral changes. That's the problem when you book meetings two years in advance. Pastors do leave. One time we got to a city only to find that the pastor had resigned and left town a few days earlier. Then we had nowhere to go.

Well, it was Christmas, and we were at the crossroads of decision out in Western Canada. No church wants an evangelist at Christmas time, and it didn't seem wise to head for California. As we closed the Edmonton meeting, we met Pastor Ken Bombay. He pastored a strong church in Calgary. We were in a dilemma, so we asked him for advice.

Ken was a super gregarious kind of person. He invited us to spend the next two weeks of the Christmas season with him and his dear wife, Joan. We had hours and hours together to talk and visit. Ken also had a suggestion:"There are many mid-size and small churches in Western Canada that cannot get an evangelist to come. If you'll go by faith and make no demands, they'd love to have you."

Well, since we never asked for a guaranteed offering anyhow, and never even requested specific accommodations, this was no problem to us.

Gradually we moved eastward, preaching in towns along the 1500 miles of Trans Canada Highway. One of the last meetings we had was in a tiny community called Rivers, Manitoba. It wasn't even on our map. The building was full night after night, in spite of the sub-zero weather.

In our meetings, I'd usually ask the pastor to designate one night's offering for our overseas crusade ministry. We had invitations for an entire year in Southeast Asia. But we had never set a date because we lacked most of the needed funds. However, in a small church, in a tiny community, in sub-zero weather, we received a huge missionary offering. I remember calling my dad and saying, "We're headed for Asia in three months." Yes, we still lacked much support, but I knew if God could supply so well through such a tiny church at the end of the world, He would certainly supply the remainder.

When the Rivers meeting concluded, I had one final night in Brandon, Manitoba, forty miles away. This would be a night where I almost lost my life again. The weather was bad, Heather was tired, and the pastor's family encouraged her not to go. Since it was a meeting for men and boys, that made good sense. In Brandon I had a wonderful dinner with Dick and Vera Wilding from Trinidad. We'd had a share in leading them to the Lord when we were in the city five months earlier.

After the church service in Brandon, I phoned back to Rivers. The pastor promised to meet me at a crucial crossroads to be sure that I'd not miss the turn. Well, I'd hardly reached the edge of Brandon when the snowfall became heavy. Then on the radio came the message, "The RCMP warns of a severe blizzard. No one should be on the highway until further notice!"

I'd heard similar warnings in Tennessee, but this was different. I thought, well, instead of driving 60 miles an hour, I would just drive 30 or 40. Still, I'd be in Rivers in just an hour or so. As I drove, the storm worsened. I debated turning back, but I knew the pastor would be waiting for me at the junction. Anyhow, there was no space to turn around on the narrow road. Soon I couldn't even see the edge of the road. The snow was up to the sides of the small highway, and there were no shoulders.

Finally, I was creeping at only five miles an hour or less. I could not see ten feet ahead of me. When I'd feel the tires go off the edge of the road, I'd gradually turn to the other side. This went on for what seemed like an eternity.

Then I passed right by the junction sign—fortunately I didn't hit it. The pastor was to meet me there, but I didn't see him. With the visibility being only ten feet, I got out of the car to search. I frantically called to him. I wondered, had he run off the road or had he frozen to death in the sub-zero weather? At least the pastor would know every turn and curve of the road on the way to Rivers, so maybe he was okay. I desperately hoped so.

By now, my gas was getting dangerously low and the engine was starting to overheat. I almost ran over the embankment as I turned onto the road to Rivers. Putting the windows down, I leaned out to try to see better. Soon my face was numb with cold, and I was numb with fear. I'd heard of people freezing to death in blizzards. Now it appeared I would have a chance to see how that could happen.

Finally, ahead, I saw the first car I had seen all night. What a relief—it was the pastor, who had safely driven this road hundreds of times. Now all I had to do was follow his taillights—very closely. Before long, we were home. I did thaw out. My face was not frostbitten. God was merciful once again, and yes, it was wonderful to be "sponsored by the Holy Spirit."

20

BIBLE SMUGGLER

A Burmese jail did not particularly appeal to us. Yet the missionary on the phone was insisting that we take (smuggle) Bibles into this hostile country. My first response was "No way!"

He explained, "Burma is closed to the gospel. All missionaries have been expelled and the churches are being persecuted. No one is allowed to take Bibles into the country. Many of our believers don't have a single copy. And even worse, at our Bible school, all of them are kept in the library. The students must check them out for their studies. And you are the only ones who have permission to enter the country."

I glanced at little Deborah, and then asked Heather, "What do you think? You know it's risky."

The timing could not have been worse. We had been travelling over Southeast Asia for five months. The services in Bangkok had concluded just the night before. Not only were we weary, but Heather and I both had contracted what was called dengue fever. This fever is caused by mosquito bites, and brings fever, severe muscle aches, fatigue and nausea.

The next morning we were to fly to Rangoon, Burma (Myamar). Because of the fever we could barely pack our own clothes. As fast as we dragged something into the suitcase, two-year-old Deborah pulled it out. How could we worry about carrying Bibles? And even if we did, the extra weight seemed overwhelming.

In spite of the risk, we agreed to take ten Bibles. I figured we could stash them around in our five pieces of luggage. Then the missionary arrived with two large boxes. One box contained about 50 Bibles. The other contained car parts, clothes, etc. This would put us way over the weight allowance. And how do you hide 50 Bibles?

Our interest in Burma went back two years earlier. Not only had the government expelled all missionaries, but no outsiders were allowed visas. There was a single weekly flight from Bangkok to Calcutta. This required an overnight stay in

Rangoon, the capital of Burma. But even this required a special permit. The country was controlled by a repressive, communist dictatorship.

The believers met our plane on our first visit and took us immediately to the church. The people were thrilled to see someone from the outside world. Their world was like a prison. The meeting was saturated with the presence of the Lord. After church, we talked late into the night with our hosts. They were eager for world news, as all communications into the country were blocked.

Reluctantly, we said goodbye the next morning and boarded the flight for Calcutta. The sky looked ominous. As we took off, the wind picked up, and the turbulence tossed our plane almost out of control. I was terrified, but Heather had fallen asleep. I shook her awake so that we could be scared together.

Before long, the pilot told us we'd flown into the headwinds of a typhoon and there was no way to continue. So the plane turned around and flew back through heavy turbulence for another two hours.

After a safe landing, we contacted the church. They were so excited they scheduled another special service. And that afternoon some of the folks took us to an amazing Buddhist temple complex of marble streets and gold-covered idols.

As we left the next morning, we felt deep concern for the oppressed Burmese people.

Needless to say, two years later, we were anxious to revisit the folks in Rangoon. Seven-day visas could now be obtained, but what about the 50 Bibles and car parts, etc.?

The Union Of Burma Airways crew had mercy on us and overlooked the excess weight of our luggage. But the flight was nerve-wracking. Not only were we both sick, but we sat beside an emergency exit door that would not totally close. For the three-hour flight the wind squealed through the crack beside us. And we were nervously looking ahead to facing Burmese customs officials with illegal goods in our possession. Burmese jails, we'd heard, were little better than torture chambers. Some Asian countries even put children in jail with the parents, I guess to preserve family unity.

Tension mounted as we landed and waited for our luggage to arrive. Debbie was tied on Heather's back, Chinese fashion, to leave her hands free for the carry-on baggage. Most of the Bibles were still in the cardboard box, but some were stuffed into the diaper bag under dirty baby clothes, where we thought they would be safest.

Night had fallen, and the airport terminal was nearly vacant. The only other people on our plane were Russian and Communist Bloc workers. We were definitely conspicuous.

Finally, all our bags were assembled before the grim customs agents. But their attention was on the blond little toddler strapped to Heather's back. This was the way Burmese babies were carried, which delighted them no end. As they began to examine our things, Heather set Debbie down on the box of Bibles. The agent started to examine the box. Then we spotted something previously overlooked. The Bibles were in a baby formula carton! I guess the agent noticed it and assumed the box actually contained milk for the baby. With a smile they cleared us to go on our way.

What a relief! Now we were anxious to give the Bibles to the pastor. Imagine my bewilderment when he told me we were being followed and he couldn't receive the books. He added that if the Bibles were given out during our stay, the police would trace them back to us. So you might say the Bibles were "hot."

The Moses family were our hosts. They were a little concerned about bringing the Bibles into their home. They suggested we hide them under our bed. For an entire week, I cringed with every knock on the door.

The dengue fever that had attacked us in Bangkok gradually loosened its grip. The Moses' treated our little family with loving care. The services in their church were very special. One of the young men showed up in a pair of white bell-bottom pants which were very "in" in the West at that time. His were made from a chenille bedspread, the best he could do. Heather grinned at him and gave him a thumbs up. True, most of the people had little of this world's goods, but they knew the joy of the Lord.

Eventually a European man came and got the Bibles from under our bed. We hope he escaped police detection. He said he was taking them to a Bible school and would give them to young pastors. Meanwhile, we said goodbye to our Burmese friends and moved on to be with one of the most outstanding missionary couples of our generation—Mark and Hulda Buntain in India.

21

WAS IT A WITCH'S CURSE?

Travandrum is in the southern-most region of India. India is about the size of the state of Texas. Indian Airways was on strike, so we covered most of this vast nation for three months on wood and coal-burning trains. The black soot swirled back through the open windows. In just a few hours, our faces and clothes were always literally black.

Our travel was made more challenging as our daughter, Deborah, was now a year-and-a-half. Our train had compartments with sliding doors like you sometimes see in the movies. Since Debbie was so active, Heather would wipe down the entire compartment with Detol (Indian Lysol), and then she would turn Debbie loose.

On our arrival in Travandrum, we were placed in the nicest hotel, comparable to a Motel 2 ½. The exterior was impressive, but inside there were crude furniture, bunk beds and hordes of ants.

At a nearby store we made a lucky find—two chocolate bars. We hadn't seen chocolate in months. But what about the ants? Then I had a brilliant idea. Why not suspend the chocolate by a thread from the top of the bunk beds? Then after church we'd have a long-anticipated treat.

Imagine our amazement as we returned from church. I knew ants were smart, but these Indian ants were geniuses. They not only located the candy, but they were making their way up and down the tiny thread. One of them on the back of a string would meet one ant on the front of the string; they would pause, and then help each other past the bottleneck. What cooperation! We could learn from them, but our candy was ruined.

Now, on to the witches. Our crusade was on the edge of town. An eager crowd came and sat in the open air. Each night the crowds seemed to grow. One evening, the sponsoring pastor asked us to come to his home. His little daughter was very sick. As we prayed, we noted her high fever. Yet we all believed that she would soon be okay. Imagine our shock, when the next morning we found that the little girl had died!

Someone explained, "It's the witches and the Hindu priest! This is the second time it has happened. This area is controlled by evil spirits!"

"What do you mean," I asked, "this is the second time?" They explained that the last pastor here also had a little girl. Some people hated him. His daughter took ill and died suddenly of a fever. How sad now, two pastors had lost little girls.

Expectantly, we waited for the last night of the crusade to begin. We were looking forward to over 1,000 attending. There had been some amazing testimonies of people being saved, healed and yes, some delivered from demon spirits.

Debbie, our little girl, was scurrying around as usual as we prepared for the final meeting. Then in a matter of minutes, her temperature shot up and she flopped down on the floor near comatose. Then it hit us! The last two gospel ministers had both lost little girls to a demon-inspired fever. Now Debbie was desperately sick.

At first, we prayed and quoted scripture. We rebuked the devil! Nothing changed. Then I picked up little Debbie in my arms, and began to sing and worship the Lord. It seemed the enemy wanted to destroy this final night, as well as our small family.

There were no doctors or medicines available, but we believed God would somehow see us through again. As we sang and worshiped the Lord, an amazing thing happened. Debbie's fever broke, and she began to run around again. In a matter of minutes she was completely normal.

God had once again intervened for us. We were able to go to the final night of the meetings. It was a very special night as many hundreds of people came and gave their hearts to the Lord. We look back on those days in India, grateful for the prayers of so many people that were lifting us up. Once again, we realized that this ministry was "sponsored by the Holy Spirit."

Crowd greets us on our arrival in Guam, 1970

Gene practicing pharmacy, 1963

Gene and Heather's wedding day, Toronto, Canada, 1965

Conducting Good News Crusades in Kenya, Africa, 1968

Soldiers evacuate us in Bangladesh Civil War, 1970

Deborah and Heather in army truck, Bangladesh, 1970

The Golden City—Buddhist temple complex in Rangoon, Burma, 1970

Bibles successfully smuggled into Burma, 1970

Debbie watches bear on the streets of Istanbul, Turkey, 1972

Thailand—local transportation, 1973

UTAPAO, Thailand—Servicemen's center opens, 1973

The Vine Servicemen's Center, UTAPAO, Thailand, 1973

UTAPAO, Thailand—Ice delivery, 1973

Clark Air Force Base—Philippine dress, 1975

Mom and Dad Reed by the nipa hut, Philippines, 1978

Speed-the-Light van—Thanks Tennessee! 1981

Flagellanties and Crucifixion—Philippines, 1977

Som, Deborah, and friend—Bangkok, 1984

Sunday noodle dinner—Bangkok, 1984

Deborah and Som with his RX7, 1993

Mom with Gene and Ron—2000

The Burgess brothers—Ron, Phil, and Gene, 2002

Bible distribution—Moscow, Russia, 1997

Bible school students—Mongolia, 2002

The Burgess clan—Christmas 2003

22

"WHAT A HEALING JESUS"

"What a Healing Jesus" is a song written by Mary Brown. It has often encouraged me and literally millions of others. Several times TBN Network stars Dean and Mary have ministered this song in churches we pastored. Every time I hear it, it inspires my faith. Then as I listen, I'm reminded that my life story could be chronicled by numerous times that I have been healed, my life has been spared, or we've experienced God's undeserved mercy and grace.

Before we settled as fully appointed missionaries in Thailand and the Philippines, we served as missionary evangelists. Basically, we conducted special meetings for a month in each nation as we moved from Japan all the way around to Central Asia and into Africa. During these two years of missionary journeys, many times we saw the hand of God upon us.

MALARIA IN REMOTE PHILIPPINE ISLAND—Almost "Bye Bye" For Me

Several of our Filipino missionaries made plans to make the treacherous journey from Illoilo City, Panay up to the youth camp in a place called Bye Bye. Then one by one, our missionary friends began to cancel out due to "unforeseen circumstances." I accused them of being chicken-hearted. Anyhow, we had no idea the trip involved seven hours in an open-sided bus over dirt roads. Next we took a motorbike ride, and finally a small bonca boat with bamboo outriggers up a narrow tropical river. At last, we reached the camp at Bye Bye. This trek would prove to be almost "bye bye" for me too.

At the camp was a humble chapel for the youth gatherings. We lodged with the staff in a large bamboo dwelling on stilts. One night, we counted twenty people jammed into the home sleeping on the floor.

Halfway through the opening night, a lady interrupted me as I was preaching through an interpreter. She stood up, and in perfect English urged people to come to Jesus. Since this was what I was already attempting to do, I was a little bit irritated with her. In spite of the interruption, people did come and accept Christ that night, and we had a good service. The excited pastor later exclaimed what a spectacular service it had been. I really wasn't sure what was happening. Then he explained, the message that the lady gave was in English, and she interpreted it into the Philippine Tagalog language. But this lady knew no English, he said, and had never even been around English-speaking people. God was obviously at work.

When God begins to work, the enemy also starts working. This time I was his target. Feeling weak and feverish after service, I went to our tiny eight-foot by eight-foot room and lay down on the hard bamboo bed. Before long, the slight fever shot up dramatically. I had trouble controlling my feet and my legs. Then my whole body began to shake and convulse.

Malaria was rampant in this area. Remembering this and our treacherous journey, I understood why my missionary companions had canceled the trip!

There were no doctors or medicines within miles. I had become delirious as Heather called for the pastors living in our native hut to come and pray. I only got worse. They came the second time and prayed, but again I was worse. Finally they came for the third time. I frantically pleaded with them, "You must touch God for me, my fever is soaring and I can't control the trembling in my body." After this third prayer, I slipped into a deep sleep. The next morning I awoke refreshed and ready to carry on full blast. The Lord had been merciful and healed me.

Following this youth camp, we were scheduled to take a six-hour trip in the open ocean by outrigger canoe from Kalibo, Aklan to the rocky island of Romblon. When the Filipino pastor came to take us on the journey, I almost backed out. A one-hour trip up a river is one thing, but six hours in the open ocean on a small outrigger seemed too risky to me. I told the pastor there was no way we would go unless Heather and I had life preservers. These folks had never even heard of life jackets. However, I did tell them we'd settle for two inner tubes. But I explained, if this boat went down, Heather and I would get the inner tubes and were not going to share them with anybody else. If they wanted to stay alive, they all ought to get an inner tube. Well, there were only two inner tubes on the little craft when it arrived.

Even though we had rented it ourselves, the mayor of Romblon Island decided he wanted to go along for free. He also brought along a few of his friends. So we were jammed so tightly together, we were hardly able to move for the entire trip. The sharks followed us on the journey.

Romblon had not seen a missionary in years. We stayed in a house on stilts with the usual scratching and grunting of pigs and chickens underneath. Because there was no electricity or running water, I shaved outside over a basin. My mirror hung from a palm branch. Crowds of kids gathered to watch the "operation" every morning. But we met scores of precious Filipino people. Some had walked for miles to attend the evening crusades. Many, many people came to know Jesus, and the dangerous six-hour journey was worthwhile.

MALARIA ATTACKS AGAIN

Several weeks later, we were ministering on the island of Java in Indonesia. Missionary Anthony Sorbo was our coordinator. What a fervent commitment the youth on the Island of Java had. In those days, we focused primarily on young people. In fact, in Southeast Asia, most of the churches in that period of time were composed of energetic youth.

Missionary Sorbo drove us from the airport in the capital of Djakarta to Malang. We crossed the entire island of Java, 600 miles in 18 hours. He insisted on driving at night when it was cooler. We were nervous about doing this on very poor third-world highways.

That night about 2 a.m., Anthony slammed on his brakes. We barely missed a huge sugar cane truck stopped right in the middle of the highway. The driver was underneath the truck asleep. He had no lights on, but he had put a tree branch behind the truck to show he was stopped. It was a close call.

A CIA AGENT?

Anthony Sorbo did not like to stop, but finally at midday we got a break. I was ready for some picture taking, so he allowed me an hour for photos. Just down the street I was excited to see a large Indonesian Army Camp. There had been fierce fighting going on between the government and the Communist guerillas in the area. I asked the guard at the gate if I could take his picture. He smiled and posed. Usually photos like this could get you into trouble. But I had his permission; at least I thought I had his permission.

Just inside the gate, I saw some tanks and troops marching. I thought these would make good photos as well. A couple of Indonesian Army Officers approached me, and they posed as I also took their pictures. I thought everything was cool. Then they graciously invited me to come into the camp to see the base commander. These folks were cordial indeed.

The next thing I knew, I was in the Commanding General's office. After some pleasantries, he demanded, "Why are you here working for the CIA?" He continued in an unpleasant tone, "We have never seen a spy walk right into our base and take photos in broad daylight. You are very bold and brazen." My knees began to knock. Yes, it appeared I had been most unwise—there are other words to explain my actions.

I honestly told the interrogators about our ministry and that I was with a recognized Indonesian missionary only a few blocks away. They weren't convinced, but in a few minutes in walked Anthony Sorbo with a military escort. Anthony verified my story. I didn't go to jail. But the things Anthony said to me when it was over were not very pleasant!

Indonesia is composed of about 6,000 islands. It is the largest Muslim nation on earth. Most of the people live in overcrowded slums and earn little more than $1.00 a day. But when the Christian believers gather to worship, oh how they sing and praise the Lord. They've found great riches in Christ.

During our six weeks in Java, we spoke in large churches of over 1,000, in small house churches, in Bible schools, open-air crusades and youth camps.

WHERE ARE THE DOCTORS WHEN YOU NEED THEM?

The second malaria attack came near the time for our departure from Indonesia to Singapore. I had been warned that the malaria that had attacked me in the Philippines could recur at any time. For many, any change of weather or even altitude could bring a fresh wave of this life-threatening disease.

We were ministering in a youth camp in Central Java. There were plenty of mosquitoes. But the local missionary told me on our arrival not to worry, malaria was not a problem. Can you believe, the next day he came down with malaria himself?

The youth camp was electric with excitement. The young people even had their own Speed-The-Light missionary projects. They were raising money to buy bicycles for local pastors. One night they rode a bicycle to the platform. Everyone came forward and pinned rupiah (Indonesian money) all over the spokes of the bike. These poor teens gave the equivalent of several hundred dollars. This deeply moved Heather and me as we gladly joined in the giving.

Our accommodations were bare survival. In fact, for most of the 12 months overseas on this trip, we were lodged in some pretty horrid places. The place where we stayed was run by the local Indonesian Government as a service to poor travelers. Our room cost 35 cents a night! We were overcharged! Sometimes we referred to our lodging places as the Motel 2 ½.

I teasingly grabbed what I thought was the best bed in the room and gave Heather the other. But soon I began to itch all over. Finally I jumped up—bed bugs! Our traveling companions were equipped with DDT. So with a coating of DDT over the mattress, we lay down again. Heather had the last laugh because her bed had no bed bugs.

Just a few minutes after we lay down to sleep, I began to feel hot. In the tropics, it rarely gets below 80 degrees even at night. But I had a fever. Soon my legs began to twitch. Then my left arm started trembling. I tried to be calm and not mention it until both arms and my whole body went into convulsions. The malaria had returned worse than ever!

There were no doctors or medicines. We were in a run-down "hotel" called a losman with nobody to help. This time there was no band of Filipino pastors praying. It was up to Heather and me alone. I pleaded with Heather to pray, because I suddenly had more fear than faith. Heather fully realized the gravity of the situation. As she began to pray, almost instantaneously my limbs stopped shaking. The fever dropped, and energy flowed into my body. I'll never forget walking outside in the night air and gazing into the heavens. It was as if I had gotten my life back.

Some cautioned that as we traveled to various countries with different climates, I could expect the malaria to return. But that's been over 35 years ago. We've been in scores of malaria-infested areas, but it has never returned. The only reminder I had of the Indonesian malaria episode was that for several days I still had tiny whelps from the bed bugs. Heather taunted me, saying it was simply because I was hogging the best bed. Maybe she was right and I got what I deserved.

23

I'M GLAD SHE WOKE UP

After nine months of constant travel in crusades in Southeast Asia, we accepted the post as interim pastor in Guam. One day, as I went to the downtown post office in Agana, the capital of Guam, I met Brother David Berg. He was more seasoned in the ministry than I was. In Guam we'd seen wonderful revival. Also, we had seen some odd behavior. Old-time ministers called it "wild fire." Though some declare, "wild fire is better than no fire," it can be destructive.

For about three weeks, every time we gathered at the altar to pray and seek an outpouring of the Holy Spirit, several youth would begin to scream as if in great pain. It was distracting and frightening. I know that every true and genuine revival has some extremes. And usually when people are distracted by the extremes, the revival can be discredited.

So after a disturbance on a Sunday night, I was glad to meet an older, Spirit-filled minister on that Monday morning. As I told Dave what was happening, he gave me some interesting advice. We had been rebuking the devil during these intrusions and this satanic-like influence. "I believe you have some sincere youth who love attention," Dave said. "They aren't really seeking God, but are looking for emotion. The more you pray for them, the worse they get. So why not just ignore them and pray with others. I believe it will stop."

Guess what—he was right. The disturbances stopped, and genuine seekers found the Lord. Waves of blessings continued to flow, and countless others were saved and filled with the Spirit.

One day Brother Dave told me about his previous mission work in the Solomon Islands. The Solomons were about 3,000 miles southeast of Guam—really in the middle of nowhere. He had seen hundreds of people saved and scores baptized in water. Many signs and wonders had occurred. I listened spellbound. Then he told me, with tears in his eyes, that the government had expelled him and all other missionaries. He was forbidden to return. In my spirit, I determined to go there one day. But no ministers were allowed visas.

As our interim pastorate in Guam was nearing completion, the desire to preach in the Solomons increased. Since I was truly a registered pharmacist, I used that background to apply for permission to visit. With permission granted, our family had to be split up for about six weeks. Heather and little Deborah boarded the plane for the States, and I left for the Solomon Islands.

My flight to get to the Solomons was long and complicated. First, I had to fly to Manila, Philippines and lay over, then on to Port Moresby, New Guinea, and lay over. Finally, there was an eight-hour hop across several south Pacific islands on a small, twin-engine aircraft.

On our journey, we stopped in New Hebrides. The "air terminal" was only a little shack on the edge of a thick jungle. We were really in a very remote place. I noticed something dripping from the plane. Being concerned about the loss of fluid and our remote location, I asked the pilot about it. "Oh," he said, "it is only hydraulic fluid. We'll put some more in. No problem." Well, we had still four more hours of open ocean. As you can see, we did make it, as I am writing this account.

On arrival at the small Honaira, Solomon Island airport, I went through immigration procedures. The officer in charge gave me a strange look. "You sure look familiar. Is this your first visit here?" he inquired. "Somehow your face is fixed in my mind." Then it hit him, "Oh you're the man whose picture is all over the island. You've come to preach a Good News Crusade!"

Well, I kind of had "stammering lips" and replied that it was true, but that I was a pharmacist by education. I understood all missionaries were expelled, but I had come to "just bring greetings from America." Permission to enter was granted, but the police watched my every move. Every night the police surrounded the area where we were conducting our open-air meetings in a thatched roof building.

All went pretty well, until one morning I took very ill. My fever went out of control. No medical help was available. It was miserably hot in the humble pastor's home where I was staying. As my strength ebbed away, I began wishing for home, Heather, air-conditioning and an American doctor. Sickness away from home in primitive surroundings is frightening. The pastor and his wife joined in prayer for my healing, and my condition, though grave, did stabilize.

As the evening service time approached, a miracle happened. Somehow, fresh strength and energy surged through my body. I was able to get up and preach—rather "bring greetings from America." Again, many came to know Jesus that night. And again, the police had surrounded the outside of the thatched roof tabernacle.

Now the rest of the story. When I returned to the USA, there was a strange phone call. Mrs. Alice Shaffer Blythe was on the line. She undoubtedly is one of the great women of faith and prayer in our generation. She inquired if I'd been sick recently while overseas. Then the story unfolded. "One night," she related, "I had a strange dream. It was about you, Gene. There was an ugly creature that had a hold on you. This monster was choking out your very life. I awoke and began to pray and cry out to God for you. As I pled for God to intervene, after awhile I felt peace." She asked the date and time of my illness and recovery. It was exactly the time God had woken her up! The key thought here is that I'd like to stay close enough to God that He could awaken me, even in the wee hours of the morning, and impress me to pray for someone. When we are led by the Spirit to pray, miracles happen.

24

"DEADLY" PINEAPPLE

Many major events of my life could be told by simply sharing the times the Lord has healed and protected me from danger. You would not normally think that pineapple juice could be harmful, would you?

After three months in Guam, I set out alone for six weeks of crusades across the South Pacific. First, there was ministry in the Solomon Islands. Next, I boarded a rickety two-engine plane for Suva, Fiji. All of these islands are tiny dots on a map, separated by hundreds of miles of open ocean.

In the Suva area, I spoke at several large, thriving churches and in newer, pioneering ministries as well. Also, I taught in our Bible school. This was the first time I had lodged and had my meals with the local native students. In the tropical heat, we had one tiny fan. The students did the cooking. I'd rate the cuisine between horrible and terrible. It really bothered my stomach. The missionary did invite me to his lovely home for one meal. A real generous fellow.

The next destination was on another island about two hours away by plane. The plane resembled something from the dark ages. As we landed, all I could see were acres and acres of pineapple fields.

The Fijian pastor and his wife who met me were so gracious. When we reached their neat but humble home, they handed me a large glass of cold pineapple juice. I was soaked in sweat and so thirsty. Momentarily, I forgot about the stomach pains—cramping, burning, nausea and periodic weakness. Anyhow, I gulped down the entire large glass. Within moments, I knew it was a mistake. Overcome by stomach pain and weakness, I immediately had to go to bed. The pineapple juice with its high acid content was like poison to my system.

You can be sure I felt foolish, having come this far and ending up in bed before the very first service. Somehow, I dragged myself out of bed and to church that night. Leaning on the pulpit, I preached, or I tried to preach. Then it was back to bed. The next night I was even weaker, but I still made myself go on. By the third night, I was so weak that I could hardly stand up.

The meetings had to be canceled. I flew back to the capital city of Suva. The missionaries were too busy to meet me, but offered me a room at the Bible school again. I had already been there and done that. For once, I declined my lodging offer and got a nice air-conditioned hotel room.

I cancelled the next crusades on the island of Tonga, some 600 miles away. My tickets were rerouted for the quickest way back home to the USA. The flight was eerie. It was on a new four-engine jet operated by American Airlines. But the route was only two weeks old and under-used at this time. We flew over 1,000 miles up to Samoa on a 130-passenger plane with only four people on board. Did the people who chose not to fly know something we didn't?

How good it was to finally touch down in Memphis some twenty hours after leaving Fiji. Heather and the kids were at the airport with my folks. That was a "glad reunion day." When the euphoria dimmed, the pain returned. I was taking so much medicine, it's a wonder I could function.

This ulcer problem first had popped up while we were in Bombay, India some months before. One night, while in the pulpit there I got deathly sick. I had to leave the service and coughed up a lot of blood. Afterwards, every once in awhile, this problem seemed to come back. But now, things were really grim. The pain and weakness kept me confined to bed.

Depression soon followed. I was in my mid-thirties at this time, in the prime of life, with an old man's stomach. *Is my ministry over?* I wondered.

We had to go to Springfield, Missouri a couple of days later. Our Assemblies of God has special orientation classes for missionaries—the School of Missions. Heather drove the 300 miles to Springfield from Memphis.

Fran and Barker Harrison opened their home to us. Both of these dear friends had their PhD degrees. They were zealous, Spirit-filled college professors. When they lived in Memphis, and I was in town, I loved to pray at the altar. Fran and "Sister Gaither" would often come by and lay their hands on my shoulder to pray. So often, as I was traveling, their prayers refreshed me.

It was God-ordained that we be with Fran and Barker in their lovely new home. Time and again, Heather and I had prayed that I would be delivered from this debilitating ulcer affliction. But there was no miracle, no recovery, no answer. Have you ever felt that way?

Soon after our arrival, Barker asked, "How long has it been since you had a good steak?" In the past five weeks, I had been in the Solomons and Fiji. There had been plenty of bananas, papaya and pineapple, but no steak.

They took us to the best steak house in Springfield. What a wonderful meal, plus great fellowship with such dear friends. However, by the time I got home, my stomach pain returned far worse than ever. Then it dawned on me why I hadn't eaten steak for months. Not only was it not available, but I was on a soft food diet.

The pain was so bad that I was actually writhing in the bed. Urgently I called for Heather, Fran and Barker to pray. It felt as if I had actually eaten jagged glass. They prayed and left the room. Not long after, I asked them to come back and pray again. Still no relief. Paralyzing fear gripped me. *How can I go on? Is my ministry finished?* I cried to the Lord. Finally, I pled with them to come back for the third time to pray.

At this point in time, the positive confession movement was very popular. Some who were of that opinion believed it showed doubt if you ever prayed for anything more than once. They even used some scripture out of context to validate this. In fact, they believed God would have to do what you "positively confessed" or He would be embarrassed! Can you imagine actually embarrassing God?

We had already prayed twice, but I literally begged them to come back a third time. I'm not sure how much faith I had, I was hurting so bad. Some think three strikes and you're out. But the third attempt was what it took to get a miracle. It was a feeling similar to when the Lord healed me of the arthritic spine condition in the Philippines. Something like warm oil seemed to flow over my stomach. In two minutes, all the pain left! Total healing had come. I literally jumped out of bed. That's been over 30 years ago. Steak, tacos, hot sauce, and yes, pineapple juice, are a delight to eat now. The message here is: pray for a miracle, and then don't give up. Pray again. Matthew 7:7 means, "Ask and keep on asking" until God answers prayer. Never give up. Keep praying for your miracle.

25

NO, HE'S NOT DRUNK!

As I was wheeled unconscious into the emergency room, the doctor immediately asked Heather if I was drunk. I'd been out cold for nearly 45 minutes. Heather exclaimed, "Of course he's not drunk. He's a preacher!"

The doctor exclaimed, "So what does that have to do with it?"

The last thing I remember was standing behind the pulpit in our chapel, singing. Feeling weak and dizzy, I started to sit down. Instead I collapsed on the floor. Some of the servicemen got me into a car and raced to the UTAPAO Air Force Base hospital. Although I was a civilian, they put me in a ward and began to run tests to see what was wrong.

The hospital ward was interesting. In the beds nearby were men injured in the Vietnam War. Some had simply been injured in bar room brawls. Others were recovering from drug overdoses. My bed was next door to a psychiatric ward. Yes, they had some very interesting people in the hospital. And I wondered if they had plans to move me next door, too.

For some reason, one of the characters in the psychiatric ward stole my glasses. Since first grade I had struggled because of poor vision. My left eye is blind, and my right can only be corrected to 20/40. Well, when somebody stole my glasses in the hospital, I developed a violent headache on top of the dizziness.

Finally I was diagnosed with hypoglycemia (low blood sugar). They warned me it was incurable and would cause weakness the rest of my life.

On my return to our center, "The Vine," I was too weak to walk. The next day I had a visitor I'll never forget. A fellow missionary, Bruce Mumm, took the time to drive three hours from Bangkok to see me. I don't remember a word he said, but his presence meant a great deal. After a brief chat with Heather, he announced, "You're going on a vacation! I'm going to take you to a missionary guest house on the beach of Hua Hin." Being kind of unreasonable and still weak, I whispered, "I can't go, they need me here. The work is too fragile to be left." Was it ego or true concern?

Obviously, I was useless to the work, but I was overcome by worry. The English Language School had grown from three to an enrollment of 200. The Lord had given us a Thai "Timothy" to pastor this group. The servicemen's group now reached nearly 100 men in attendance—100 men was a pretty good number. Maybe I began to think the work was about me and I thought I was indispensable. And maybe I'm not the only one who has ever felt this way—that the work depended on me?

Bruce would not listen to my protest but told Heather to pack a bag for me. It was a struggle to get dressed and down the stairs to the car. As darkness fell, the three of us headed down the "bomb road" on the way to Bangkok.

Why is it so many people think that ministry is about preaching good sermons? At this point I did not need a sermon, I just needed someone to get involved in my life and care and help me. There's an old saying, "Little things mean a lot." What Bruce did meant a lot!

The bomb road was specially built to carry bombs from a harbor to the B52 bombers stationed on the base. The wide road was smooth, so we could make good time. As we whizzed along in Bruce's little blue Datsun station wagon, I wondered if it was over for me. The doctors were not encouraging about my hypoglycemia.

Suddenly, it was almost over for all three of us. Our headlights caught a dark object blocking the road. Just in time, Bruce braked hard and swerved. We barely missed a big tractor with a plow that was about head-high, with no lights on it. God was merciful once again.

The next morning in Bangkok, Bruce took me to get new glasses. Again, he spent the day taking us to the modest but comfortable rest home for missionaries on the white sandy beaches of Hua Hin. The two weeks there were just "what the doctor ordered," as my mom would have said.

One big concern I had in leaving our servicemen's center was the finances. Brother Lou Harris was the lay leader of our ministry. Lou was one of the great men I've known. A tall, slender, black brother, Lou had a contagious smile. As the work began to grow, he often would declare, "This is the Lord's doing, and it is marvelous in our eyes!" Lou and I made a great duet. We agreed on most every point of doctrine and ministry, except one—tithing. Lou felt the men should give if they felt like it, or "as they felt led." When he spoke like this, I shuddered because it was unbiblical.

The men were generous, the center was self-supporting, and we sponsored several missions projects in Thailand. In fact, one man told me that God had prompted him to go beyond the tithe. He regularly gave 50% of his income. I asked him the reason for this. I thought it was more than he should be giving. The young airman explained, "Usually I was broke two days after payday. All my money went to the bars, prostitutes and drug dealers. But now that I have Jesus, I don't need these things anymore. So you see, I can give 50% of my salary and still have a lot more money than before." In spite of the generosity of a few, I felt the Bible pattern of tithing was important, and if men gave beyond that in offerings, fine. But Lou did not agree.

We returned back to UTAPAO two weeks later. It was great to see Som and Deb. We had missed them so much. We were grateful for the tender care they received from our newly converted Buddhist maid, Biah. Brother Lou was preaching the night of our arrival. By that time I had nearly recovered.

Lou's sermon startled me—"Tithing." Once the service ended, I met Lou in the office. I questioned him, "Why did you preach something you've always opposed?"

Well, he explained it this way. "As I sat in your office I noted the bills as they came in. The higher the stack of bills got, the more I prayed. Then one day as I was reading my Bible, the answer to our financial needs seemed to be, not for a few men to be overly generous, but for everybody to tithe!"

What good came out of this health crisis? Often Romans 8:28, "And we know that in all things God works for the good of those who love Him…" seems like a cruel joke. But even the unbelievers declare, "Every cloud has a silver lining."

During this time, I learned once again that nobody is indispensable, including myself. Also, our men learned to lean on the Lord and they took fresh ownership for the ministry. (Because after all, this ministry was "sponsored by the Holy Spirit.")

26

THE BOB MORTON STORY

Storms are uninvited and unwelcome. Sometimes storms howl through our lives when we're least prepared. Yet someone has said, "You can wring your hands, or you can let the storms blow you into the arms of Jesus!"

Have you ever felt empty and spiritually numb? Sure, most of us have. But it's unacceptable when you're a missionary in a war zone. You're supposed to bring a word of encouragement to war-weary airmen. During the Vietnam War, American B52 bombers rattled our windows as they made their daily forays from Thailand into North Vietnamese territory. One evening before speaking to our men at UTAPAO Bomber Base, I made a providential stop at the post office. We knew the Lord had called us to Thailand, but the hassles we encountered nearly overwhelmed us.

We had arrived in UTAPAO through an amazing sequence of events. We had changed our plans to pastor in the States and accepted a three-month assignment to our Bangkok Christian Servicemen's Center. The center was a refuge for military men fresh from Vietnam on R & R.

Then our Mission told us about 10,000 U. S. military men 100 miles south of Bangkok at UTAPAO. This place was infamous—not even a city outside the base, just shacks, piles of garbage, crime and debauchery. With a little pressure from our mission's chairman, we agreed to take a look. Shocked to see young men stumbling out of the bars at midnight, we prayed, "Oh Lord, this is a real mission field. Please get hold of someone and give them a burden for these men." Well, the Lord answered prayer. He sent us!

Our first home was sandwiched between a bar and a row of brothels. Flies buzzed over a garbage dump behind us, and the monks chanted from a Buddhist temple across the highway in front. Our finances did not allow for a refrigerator; in fact, there was no power for either an air-conditioner or a refrigerator and no money for a vehicle. Our limited electricity to run lights came from an extension cord from the bar next door. My wife, Heather, washed diapers by hand for our two children, Deborah and Som. We set up a ping-pong table and a library, and served sodas and meals to American military men who dropped by.

Do you know how you're called to preach? Anyone can preach to 3,000, but some nights we only had three. Our vision was to see our military men saved and then reaching out to local Thai Buddhists. For 2000 square miles, there was no other gospel witness to the local people. By the grace of God, through a Holy Ghost revival, our servicemen's group gradually grew. Excitement was mounting. By the time of this story, the men's group had reached about 100. These men taught the Thai people in an English language school using simple Bible stories. Eventually, the school birthed three self-supporting churches. They are still thriving today, even after the U. S. forces pulled out and the Vietnam War ended.

Yes, many good things happened. But fatigue had set in on my wife, Heather, and me. Our home—The Vine Servicemen's Center—was open ten hours a day, six days a week. Every six weeks the government demanded we leave the country. So we frequently fled to Laos, Cambodia or Vietnam to renew our visas.

Hot, humid, debilitating weather was the norm in Thailand. The Viet Cong were a constant threat. Also, numbers of men had been robbed, shot and knifed in our area. Pressures mounted! Then it happened. I collapsed from the bout with hypoglycemia mentioned earlier.

By God's grace, I fully recovered but was extremely discouraged. While enroute to speak to the men's group that had grown so miraculously, I stopped at the post office. I was despondent and weary at this time, wondering if it was really worth it. One letter I received was postmarked "Chicago." It was from Owen Carr, pastor of the great Stone Church. Over the years, we had often ministered at this wonderful church. Pastor Carr's opening words to me in the letter were, "I'm writing today to encourage you!" Wow! Was that a timely message! His letter chronicled an amazing story that started unfolding during our last visit to Chicago nearly two years earlier.

In the Chicago crusade two years earlier, we were amazed to find that some people living near the church didn't know much about it, although the area had been canvassed. As we often did, we encouraged the church people to go out and visit their neighbors and prayerfully invite them to the revival meetings. The Lord honored this simple outreach approach. As usual, Heather and I visited the homes in the two or three blocks around the church. That afternoon, we'd finished our rounds except for one last house. From the sidewalk in front of the house, we could hear the sound of acid rock music.

With a little hesitation, we knocked at the door. The walls seemed to vibrate. The door swung open. There stood a bedraggled, wild-looking, stoned young man. Bob Morton invited us into his "studio." His rock band had played in various nightclubs in Chicago, he told us. His dad owned a liquor distributorship. No one in the family had any spiritual roots. We listened to Bob talk about his band and his dream to make it big. We briefly shared what Jesus had done in our lives and invited him to the Stone Church two blocks away.

I'd just started preaching on the final night of the meetings in Chicago. In came this wild-looking young man in shorts and shower flip-flops. It was Bob! My first thought, "Oh Lord, don't let the ushers throw him out." But as he made his way toward the front, he was greeted by smiles. He didn't respond to the altar call, but walked around people praying, just looking at everyone. "Cool man, I have never seen anything like this before! I've heard a priest chant," he said. "But I've never seen people so sincere."

Pastor Carr showed such compassion to the haggard-looking young man. He presented Bob with a new Living Bible. Bob sat down and started to read. "Hey," he exclaimed, "I can understand this a h—of a lot better than the one my parents once had."

Often, we wondered about and prayed for this unusual young man who seemed so open. The time had come for us to return to Thailand. We wondered if Bob would continue going to church, and would the church have enough grace to accept him?

Two years had gone by and then came the letter from Pastor Carr at one of the lowest points in my life. "Do you remember Bob Morton, the young hippie, the guy that came to church half stoned?" Immediately, the events flooded my mind.

Now the real shocker. "I thought you'd be encouraged to know, Bob has continued faithful. Not only has he been saved, but also he has led his sister to the Lord and one of the band members has also been saved. All three of them are now in Bible school together."

The news, so unexpected and thrilling, left me numb. God had answered prayer! And at a point of near despair in my life, He inspired a brother to write me about a miracle I only had a tiny part in. All of a sudden, I had a testimony and a sermon for the men in the base chapel that night. My faith had received a shot of "soul tonic."

Time and again, the Lord reminded me of his faithfulness. Eventually, we returned to the U.S.A. and once again were in Chicago at Stone Church for their great annual Missions Convention. One night, just before I spoke, Pastor Carr briefly mentioned the link between home and foreign missions. He then invited someone up to the platform. He was big, handsome, muscular, well-groomed, and dressed in a nice business suit. The pastor turned to me and asked, "Gene, do you know this man?" I sheepishly had to say no. "This is Bob Morton. He's about to enter full-time ministry." And again I found it true; this ministry was "sponsored by the Holy Spirit."

27

SAVED BY THE SWEET POTATO MAN

Norm was one of those former military men that sought to get lost in Thailand. He even threw away his passport and all of his identification. A powerfully built man with a black belt in karate, he was a bit intimidating.

His hero was some movie character who could climb walls and cling to the ceiling with his bare hands—"the human fly." Norm prowled through the center climbing imaginary walls, or tripping an imaginary foe and tossing him over his shoulder. Yes, he was a bit "different."

Norm had to hustle now to get money. As he started attending services at The Vine, our servicemen's center at UTAPAO, he found we served two free meals a day. Also, he found soft-hearted people who loaned him money, which he seldom repaid.

Heather was extra kind to this lonely black fellow. Her compassion has always been great for "underdogs." But when I'd nearly lose patience with Norm, she would remind me that we served a God of mercy and that's what we were supposed to share. Don't you hate it when people talk like this? I had forgotten one "minor fact"—we owed the life of our son, Som (a Thai nickname), to Norm.

But now the plot thickens. People began coming to church not only with their Bibles, but also with half-eaten sweet potato pies. They claimed they were the awfullest tasting pies and they wanted their money back—from Norm. When Heather saw this procession, she had a funny look, and I knew she had been up to something.

A neighbor told me of seeing someone sneaking into the back of our building while we were out of the country to renew our visas. They wondered what was going on. I did notice we had used a lot of bottled gas. Money from my billfold seemed to be evaporating! On our return, we also found a note from the maid that she had quit. Were the inedible sweet potato pies, the prowler at midnight, and the missing money all somehow connected? I decided to do some detective work.

Finally, the truth: my wife, Heather, and Norm had secretly gone into the sweet potato business together. The concept seemed logical to her. Norm needed money, couldn't work locally, he was a "great cook," he had loans to repay, our kitchen was vacant at midnight, and Heather had access to a little of my money.

Unfortunately, Norm produced what some labeled as the "worst stuff they'd ever put in their mouths!" Plus, he had used all our sugar, flour, and eggs, and driven the maid crazy. But why was Heather so overly involved? Sometimes fathers underestimate a mother's love and loyalty. Heather's generosity stemmed from Norm's heroism during an earlier incident. It happened like this.

One afternoon, Heather was in the center's game room talking with Norm. A few yards away traffic roared past on the major highway that linked Thailand with Cambodia. Little Som played on the floor nearby. Suddenly, in mid-sentence, Norm bolted out the door towards the busy highway, zigzagging between speeding trucks, buses and motorcycles. He grabbed something from the double yellow line and returned with his arms around the treasure he had risked his life for—our little son, Som. Somehow Som had toddled out the screen door unnoticed, and made it to the highway. If Norm had not seen him, and run as if possessed and grabbed our son, surely he would have been crushed to death.

When Heather explained the reason for their business venture in sweet potatoes, I understood her motivation. The sweet potato man had saved our son's life. She in turn wanted to make an investment in his life.

28

"IS THIS THE LAST SUPPER?"—A CURE FOR THE FEAR OF FLYING

I've discovered a way that almost anyone can be cured from the fear of flying. I personally know the answer and will gladly share the secret.

First, I must admit to having been a white-knuckled, sweaty-palmed airline passenger for years. For me, the fear began to build traveling so much on long overseas flights. Repeatedly, wherever we were, missionaries would share with us their scariest flying stories the night before our departure for the next assignment. We never slept much on those nights.

At the check-in counter I was so worried, I would study all of my fellow passengers. If too many of them looked a bit overweight, I'd be even more concerned. Then I would investigate how much baggage they had. And if the plane was full, I worried we'd never get off the ground.

Of course, I always got a window seat, mainly because if the wing fell off, I wanted to be the first to know it! As the plane taxied for take-off, I often pondered my fate—some of the flights ranged from 8 to 14 hours. *My, the weight of fuel alone must be tremendous*, I would think each time.

Yet, although the engines groaned and the giant monster seemed to creep forward at a snail's pace, eventually it always picked up speed. I knew that as we approached the end of the runway, if I would raise up just a little bit out of my seat, I would lighten the load. Yes, I know that's weird.

Sometime after years of flying and many panic attacks, someone took the trouble to explain a few of the facts about flying. For instance, the pilot knows the weight of all the baggage and all the freight, as well as the weight of the fuel load. With these factors in mind, the pre-flight data tells him exactly at what point the plane should lift off the runway. Also, there is a "point of no return."

It's at this point, if the plane is not airborne, there's enough runway left to brake hard and avoid a crash.

Why did I have to fly so many years before I found out I really didn't have to lift up out of my seat to help the plane take off? (This is kind of a joke, but I really was terrified). By now, our ministry has carried us to over 140 different nations and over 50 different kinds of airlines, and on every type of aircraft. Finally, what helped me overcome my fear was periodically being invited by the captain to sit in the cockpit in what was called the jump seat on several trips. Here the pilots explained to me a great deal and my fear of flying seemed to abate. Yet a few nagging concerns remained.

Finally, a series of "near death" experiences freed me forever. One near disaster happened on a remote island in the Philippines. Heather and I had been invited to minister for a week at our Bible school in Bicole. This was a unique school. It was in a poverty-stricken region. The students barely had enough food to survive. They worked at crude homemade desks that sat on dirt floors. One student had no notebook, so he wrote class notes on the margins of old magazines someone had given him.

One bright spot helped us endure our tiny room with its dirt floor. We looked forward to going to a hotel for a good meal on the last night of our stay. The hotel was famous for serving the smallest fish in the world. When I found out you could place 10 to 15 of these tiny fish inside a bottle cap, I asked if I could have more than just one fish! Actually, the fish were made into patties and were quite tasty.

As we left the school, our hearts went out to these devoted students, who in their lifetime probably would never know any abundance. At the airport, we boarded a twin-engine Philippine Airline turboprop for our three-hour flight back to Manila. Yes, I sat by the window. It seemed to me as we took off, the props were not turning as they should. As we bounced down the improvised runway, we did get airborne. And then it happened, one propeller stopped. The plane groaned to gain altitude over a ridge of mountains.

Well, by now I knew what the pilot was supposed to do. He would tell us there had been a problem. We'd turn and go back to the airport immediately. However, the plane, with great effort, gradually climbed and continued on. After a long time of silence, the captain spoke. "You may have noticed we've lost one of our engines. But there's no worry, we'll be landing in only four hours in Manila!" Ahead lay mountain ranges and lots of ocean.

By now, all conversation in the cabin had ceased. Everyone was terrified. The silence on board was unnerving. Eventually, the cabin attendants brought us our lunch in cardboard boxes. We could see the fear in their eyes, so I thought maybe I should try to lighten the mood a little bit. As I was served a cold chicken leg, I asked, "Is this what they call the last supper?" Then I hastened to assure her that I was a man of prayer and was confident we would make it. Finally, as we cleared Manila Bay and the plane landed safely, wild applause broke out.

On another occasion, on a small Malaysian Airline, we had another unique experience. The cockpit door was left open. Inside I could see the senior British Captain who was training a young Malaysian as the co-pilot. The pilot and co-pilot got into a heated argument. The seasoned British captain said the cross winds were far too heavy for the plane to take off, while the young Malaysian insisted it was going to be okay. Back and forth they discussed it. The plane was even being buffeted while sitting on the runway. It was at that time I started to get out of my seat and holler, "Do I have a vote too?" Anyhow, we did take off flying slightly sideways into the headwind, and we made it fine.

Another reason I was no longer fearful, is in the year before I had gotten scared so bad, I really thought we were finished and was truly surprised we survived. It's like the reports you hear of near-death experiences freeing people from any further fear of death. Once you literally think you're dead, then everything else from there on is a breeze.

The turning point at which I was freed forever of fear occured on a night flight from Monrovia, Liberia to New York City. At this point, we had spent some 12 months in crusades that started in Tokyo, Japan and ended up at Christmas in Monrovia. Christmas was certainly unique in Monrovia. Numerous Santa Clauses in brown suits stood at intersections with their friends. Have you ever imagined 50 drunken, angry Santas? These Santas had no gifts for anyone. Instead they blocked traffic and pounded on cars until people gave them money. Some had long machetes and their erratic behavior was unsettling. We were relieved when the crusades were finished and we settled back in our comfortable Pan Am Jet with an all-American crew. It was so good to feel at home and secure in a sane environment.

Enroute to New York, we did have a stop-over in Dakar, Senegal on Africa's west coast. Midway to Dakar, we found there was a problem—the landing gear instrument registered a malfunction.

But no problem, I knew our American crew could handle anything. We had total confidence in their ability. Then, sitting by the window at night, I saw red fire shooting out of one of the four engines. In only a moment, fire broke out in the second of the engines, and soon fire out of the third engine. Fear paralyzed me. I knew the plane could fly on two engines. It was somewhat doubtful it could fly on one engine. But the worst was yet to come. Suddenly, I saw red flames shooting out of the fourth engine. I knew we were going to go down, that there was no way we could survive now. I thought, *Well, we're ready to meet the Lord and this is it.* We'd been faithful to do what we felt God had called us to do. I knew shortly we'd experience a true "welcome home" celebration. Yet, for some reason the plane did not lose altitude.

After seemingly an eternity, the "competent" pilot explained, "Friends, because of our landing gear problem, we had to dump off almost all of our fuel. I hope the red lights reflecting off the vaporizing fuel did not alarm you. Some may have thought it was fire." No it didn't bother us, it just scared us half out of our wits. I was so mad at the pilot for not alerting us, I wanted to punch him out.

All night, we circled over Africa, waiting for daylight and an emergency landing in Dakar. As we made the final descent, we felt even if we landed on the belly without the landing gear and no wheels, that we'd probably survive. But as we got close to the runway, the pilot turned the plane and barely missed the control tower. *Well,* I thought, *he might be a little fatigued from the long ordeal.* The plane turned around and again seemed to line up for the runway, but then swerved and missed the control tower again. Then finally, he lined up for the third try. At this point the pilot came over the intercom explaining, "We've overflown the airport tower twice so they could examine our landing gear with binoculars. Our onboard instruments were wrong, the landing gear is in place, all is well, and we should be on the ground in five minutes."

After "dying" so often, I don't totally expect to return when I leave on a trip anymore. And when we arrive safely, I am just pleased and somewhat surprised. Once you've come to the point of thinking you're going to die, nothing worse can happen. Then you just rejoice when you arrive in one piece. That's how to conquer the fear of flying.

29

"I SEE BRAIN TUMORS IN MY PRACTICE EVERY DAY!"

My lifelong friend, Dr. John Howser, examined me. He was not hopeful. I had come through some scary things, but this was the most frightening. Something strange was going on in my head. Our mission had urged me to take immediate medical leave and fly back to Memphis from the Philippines.

For some weeks, it had become increasingly difficult to read. Since I had been plagued by poor vision all of my life, I just accepted it as normal. Then one day I became disoriented and dizzy. It was different from any inner ear dizziness I had ever known. My eyes started rotating from left to right and back. I began hearing strange noises.

One of the key men in our Clark Air Force Base Church worked at the base hospital. Jim knew the guys who worked in the Eye, Ear, Nose and Throat Clinic. Even though I was a civilian, he got me in for a long series of exams.

Extensive tests showed I had some kind of a growth or tumor in my brain near the inner ear. I literally shook as I drove home from the hospital. How, could I tell Heather, Som and Deborah? Should I do the male, macho thing and just say they recommended more tests? Dare I let them know I was scared about all the things the doctor said I might face?

Sitting quietly in our church office, I scanned my life insurance policies. At that time, there wasn't much coverage. The doctors had told me this growth would probably be inoperable.

Crises force you to stop, think, evaluate and then re-evaluate. You ask yourself, what is really important in life? Toys and trinkets seem worthless. Only two things matter at a time like this—your family and your walk with God.

The doctors at Clark strongly suggested I get to the States promptly. Yet I protested. I had flown home only six months earlier to be with my dad in the last hours before he passed away. I just could not leave the family and the church so soon again. So I said I'd go in two or three months.

The doctor shook his head. "Mr. Burgess, you could be dead in two or three months!" That's when the seriousness of it hit home.

We chose not to tell the children why their dad was leaving once again for the States. The long flight from Manila to Memphis required about twenty hours. The doctor could not see me for another two days. So the next morning, Mom suggested we go shopping. Not in the mood and with jet lag, I declined. She insisted I needed a nice dark blue suit. There was pain and fear in Mom's eyes. Was she thinking this would be my burial suit?

Off we went. She said this suit was to be "special." She drove me to the finest store in Memphis, picked out the best and asked them to rush the tailoring.

Dr. John Howser was one of the most noted neurologists in Memphis. We had often had fellowship time and Bible study together at the University of Tennessee. He was in medical school while I was in pharmacy school. It was good to see an old friend. John showed deep concern as soon as he saw me. He ran several preliminary tests. Then the shocker! "Gene, I see brain tumors everyday. I'm afraid the Air Force doctors in the Philippines are correct. You have a tumor on the brain."

To confirm the earlier findings, a long battery of new tests was ordered. All day long at Methodist Hospital, tests were run. I finally came back to see John at the end of the day. As soon as I walked into his office, he seemed surprised. "You look and walk completely different, what's happened?" he inquired. All I could say was that many were praying and God had given me a deep inner sense of peace that everything was going to be okay. You know, the worst thing the devil can threaten God's people with is heaven! I was at peace, but concerned for my little family halfway around the world.

The doctor quickly rose and said, "Let's go check out all of the battery of tests." One by one he scanned them. "Nothing here, nothing here."

I could now quip, "You mean there's no brain?"

"No," John declared, "all of your tests are negative. You're eyes aren't even darting back and forth, and you seem perfectly well!"

Even though John was a good Bible-believing Methodist, we shouted together. The Lord had graciously answered prayer once again. I knew that I was undeserving of His grace, but so grateful for God's miracle power.

Dr. Howser had lined up one final series of tests for me, just to cover all bases. He asked an allergist to check me out because I was having a great deal of fatigue.

So the day before I was to fly back to the Philippines, I saw the allergist for sensitivity tests. Usually, they make 30 tiny pinpricks at a time on your back with various agents, to test what you might be allergic to. Normally this is stretched over a period of three to four weeks. But with my departure the very next day, I got the full 120 little shots in my back in a single appointment.

Departing Memphis, I felt some discomfort as the 20-hour plane trip began. With every passing hour my back became sorer with what felt like little boils. I later discovered I had 110 whelps, indicating I was allergic to 110 different allergens. It hurt me even to sit with my back against the plane seat. For most of the journey, I lay face down on the floor of the airplane. The cabin attendants thought I was drunk, so they just left me alone. Yes, I did feel very weird lying there.

Thus two weeks after leaving the Philippines, I was back home with Heather, Deb and Som and our church family. No tumor, but it took two weeks to recover from the allergy tests! (These two doctor friends would prove a great blessing to us in the next two years).

30

SURROUNDED BY COMMUNIST GUERILLAS—MINDANAO

Our plane touched down on the grass landing strip, deep in the jungle. In the distance we saw what looked like an army tank. As we taxied to a stop, we realized we were being met by a tank and a group of soldiers armed with automatic rifles. This was not the vacation we had envisioned! The idea was to have a family vacation plus ministry at the vast Spencer Coconut Plantation.

Mindanao is a large island about the size of the state of Texas. The Muslim extremists were getting more and more bold. On a couple of earlier ministry trips, we had traveled by open-sided bus over gravel roads in this area. Periodically these rebels, financed by Libya, would attack buses and cars. But you cannot be paralyzed by constant fear, and the attacks, though brutal, were infrequent. So we were not worried this time as we took the plane into the plantation.

The vacation with our two children, Som and Deborah, started when we flew 1,000 miles south of Manila to Cotabato, Mindanao. We checked into a nice hotel with a pool for the kids. Som, who was about five years of age, was ecstatic about the pool's water slide. He played on it fearlessly as long as he had his rubber ducky to keep him afloat. On one trip down the water slide, we lost sight of him. Someone screamed, "The little boy went down." Then I saw the rubber float without Som. I dove into the water, about eight feet deep, and there was my buddy near the bottom of the pool. He was okay and wasn't too frightened. Maybe he knew his dad would soon be coming to his rescue.

On our last day in Cotabato, we took the kids to visit a Muslim village that was built over the sea on stilts. The whole community stood on the edge of the lagoon in about four to six feet of water. We took a tour in a small bonca boat with bamboo outriggers on each side. After we had completed our tour, and were walking to the bus stop to catch a ride back to town, we found ourselves surrounded by local kids. These people were very primitive and had rarely seen any foreigners. They were especially curious about our pale skin and blond hair. The crowd of children got totally out of control, pinching us and pulling at our kids' hair. Soon there was a mob of about 15 to 20 shouting, pushing, and shoving. None of us were in real danger. But our children were in a state of shock, and have never forgotten the experience.

Dick Spencer had sent his private plane over to Cotabato to take the four of us to his jungle plantation. Dick had a most unusual story. His mother was one of hundreds of schoolteachers who came to the Philippines when it was under the control of the USA, following our victory in the Spanish-American War. The American government coordinator of this program was a man named Thomas. The schoolteachers became known as Thomasites. The elder Mrs. Spencer taught school for many years, and invested her salary in local property.

Her son, Dick, expanded family holdings into one of the largest coconut plantations in the Philippines. He was a very devoted Christian. Dick was also a most generous supporter of the International Correspondence Institute, now called Global University. Likewise he was concerned about the welfare of his plantation workers. So he had invited us down for a series of services to minister to the workers' spiritual needs.

Now about the tanks and soldiers. We knew there were rebel armies in some parts of Mindanao. But now we realized that the Spencer Plantation was near one of the most dangerous areas.

At any rate, with a small army to protect us, we felt that nothing could happen to us, so we were not very worried. The Spencers had a large, beautiful home set up on stilts to catch the breezes. Inside, it was surprisingly modern and equipped with their own electric plant. Here, our kids first saw a refrigerator with an ice dispenser in the door.

When Dick came to meet us, I immediately noticed the pistol at his side. A high security fence topped with barbed wire surrounded the house.

At bedtime, a series of jungle noises met our ears. We were accustomed to the roar of the fighter bombers at Clark Air Force Base. In fact, being in the jungle seemed a bit creepy. The kids were soon tucked into bed with our assurances that everything was quite safe.

In the bright moonlight at the window, however, I soon thought I saw a shadow move. Was it just the palm branches blowing in the night air? Then there was the soft pad of footsteps. Only my imagination I guess. But yes, there truly seemed to be a shadow hovering near our window. I could clearly see the silhouette of a man with a rifle. By now we were concerned—scared is more like it I guess. Yes, we prayed. After awhile the figure moved away into the vast compound. Eventually, our heartbeats slowed to normal and we drifted into an uneasy sleep.

The next morning, wild-eyed, we told our hosts what happened. The Spencers began to laugh. We didn't think any of it was very funny at all. The man we saw, they explained, was one of their house guards. He was there to protect us, not to harm us. We realized that if we'd been told about the armed guards moving around the yard at night, we'd have had no fear. This points up the value of good, clear communication. Often, we assume everybody knows what's going on, and since we are busy, we omit crucial details.

I should add that about six or eight weeks after we left the plantation, three carloads of ladies were leaving the plantation for a Women's Conference. They were all machine-gunned to death by Muslim guerillas. Still today, the island of Mindanao is torn by violence. We do need to pray for the many Christians there whose lives are threatened by Muslim extremists.

31

LET GOD USE ANYONE HE CHOOSES

Sometimes we try to imagine how the Lord will answer our prayers. And we even give God advice, telling Him how and when to obey our orders. Some even shout, "Do it now in Jesus name!" There must be a fine line between great faith and egotistical presumption.

For a period of time, as we traveled in worldwide crusades, my prayer was, "Please Lord use me as an instrument to minister to the needs of people." Then one day it hit me; God could use me, but He could also use many others as well. Finally, I became so desperate for God's mighty power to work, that I changed my prayers. I began to pray, "Lord use the worship leader, the soloist, choir, youth, seniors or anyone You choose." So the point is, we must reach a place of letting God show His power and His blessings through anyone He chooses.

Over the years, I'd forgotten this truth. But I was about to get a quick refresher. For some months, my neck and upper back hurt all the time. We were just planning an ambitious building program at the Clark Air Force Base Church near Manila, Philippines. I thought the pain was stress. Exercise and massage therapy did not help, however.

Dr. Joe Tolidano and his wife, Hazel, a nurse, were members of the church. Finally I went to see Dr. Joe. The x-rays came back showing an arthritic condition in my neck. Dr. Joe said it was a permanent thing I'd have to live with from now on. So doses of Valium, muscle relaxants and analgesics were prescribed.

There were some days that I was probably "out of it." The church was gracious. Periodically, they would joke about something rather goofy that I said if I took too many pills. But I reached a place of realizing I couldn't live on pills. Finally, like so many others, I got desperate enough to cry out to God in earnest prayer. I don't know why we seem to call on God as the last resort rather than the first resort. The church joined in prayer. Days of agony and drugs went by.

One of the members of our church was a Florida native, Wade Bryant. Every church has at least one "Wade." My first meeting with Wade was an accident, or maybe a divinely inspired appointment.

While in Thailand, we had post office (APO) privileges on the base for a short time. One day I was standing in line at the post office reading a letter. Somebody seemed to be staring over my shoulder. I turned around, and the man introduced himself to me as Wade Bryant. He inquired, "Are you really Brother Burgess?" He continued, "My mother just wrote me about you. She read about you in the Pentecostal Evangel and told me you were at the servicemen's center called The Vine."

Wade would often join the other men for the free meals at our center. But he would usually disappear before any devotionals or evening rallies. Wade loved his big cigars and the bar life. Wade had backslidden and gone far from his Assembly of God roots.

Overseas, we met hundreds who had good Bible backgrounds. Yet, the peer pressure and the lure of sin entrapped so many. Men with heartbreaking stories were regulars in my office. Some even ended up facing lengthy sentences in filthy Thai prisons.

Three weeks before Wade was to finish his tour at UTAPAO, Thailand, God shook him. He made a 180 degree turn. He was so transformed by God's power that everyone could see the difference. One day as we talked, he confessed, with tears flowing down his cheeks, to living a reckless lifestyle. He asked, "What can I do about all the men I've influenced into a godless, sinful life?" Wade turned into a redheaded, flaming evangelist. He became far more committed to God than he'd ever been committed to the devil.

With the Vietnam War winding down, we transferred from Thailand to the Philippines. Soon, we were settled in to pastoring Clark Assembly of God Church. Located across from a major gate of the base, it was mainly a servicemen's church. About 10,000 U.S.A. military personnel were stationed there. Not long after our arrival, guess who walked in—Wade. He had also been transferred to the Philippines.

Wade was still on fire for God, though maybe a little overboard in his zeal. Instead of carrying a cigar and a beer, he carried a Bible everywhere he went. He genuinely loved Jesus, but he was a bit weird. Some of his doctrine and beliefs were kind of over the edge. And he always wanted me to let him preach—a frightening thought. A pastor does have to protect the flock. You never know what some people might say in the pulpit. More than once, I've been held responsible for inappropriate remarks made by a guest speaker.

One night Wade stood up in church. He was six foot five, 250 lbs., and just took over the service. As he walked forward, he declared, "It's time for us to pray for God to heal Brudder Burgess' neck." It was hard for him to say the word "brother."

As the church gathered around me, I must admit, my faith was low. I had previously prayed to be healed. But the arthritic condition in my neck still brought constant nagging pain. As Wade approached, I thought maybe if someone more articulate and sophisticated prayed, we'd get this miracle. And I wondered, with some of his strange beliefs, would anything happen when Wade prayed? The Bible does promise, "According to your faith, be it unto you," (Matthew 9:29, KJV). My faith was low as I thought, *Oh just let him pray, it can't hurt any worse.*

God is so good—He is a God of surprises. As Wade touched my head, something like warm oil seemed to flow down my spine. Instantly, the pain and stiffness were gone. I was shocked that God could use Wade and could ignore my unbelief. I'm glad for the promise that He is able to do "exceedingly abundantly above all that we ask or think."

32

THE FLYING MACHINE &
THE NIPA HUT ON FIRE

I thought to myself, *The address must be wrong*, as I walked up and down the street. But it had to be this place called the Flying Machine.

I was trying to locate a middle aged civilian man who had come into the worship service at Clark Assembly of God one Sunday morning. I knew he was a civilian because they were the only ones that could have long hair and a beard. When the invitation was given, he had come to the altar to accept the Lord as his Savior. After we prayed, he gave us his address and asked me to visit him.

Bob's business happened to be the largest bar in the entertainment district. On walking into the Flying Machine the next day, everything was dark. I called out to him. Giggles echoed in the dimly lit background—the voices of bar girls and prostitutes.

Soon Bob appeared and seemed pleased I'd come to visit. "Here," he instructed, "have a seat at the bar. Can I get you a beer?"

I realized that this was an open-hearted man who had no real moral compass. My discomfort vanished as I recalled that the worst accusation hurled at Jesus was, "He was a friend of sinners." Bob described the peace that had come to his life as he had committed it to the Lord. He seemed so zealous. Then he volunteered, "I want to help the church with some money." I was fine with that. But then the bombshell, "Would you pray the Lord would bless my business so I can give more money to the church?" I was so shocked I could hardly speak.

Rebuke was not what Bob needed. But I did open a door of communication and fellowship with him. He kept coming to church, and we would soon see the effects of his new life in Christ.

A few days after we visited Bob in the Flying Machine, we had special dinner guests. Major Greg Wiggins was an F4 fighter pilot who had begun to date a schoolteacher by the name of Margaret Veary. He, along with Bob, had had a recent encounter with God that had dramatically changed his life. Greg and Margaret were in the mid years of life and had fallen in love after meeting at the church. Plans were being laid for their wedding.

Before supper, there were some important wedding details to be settled. So we instructed Som and Deborah to play outside. We knew the kids would soon want a drink or need to tell us something, so we gave them strict orders to stay outside. "Don't bother us for any reason for the next 30 minutes."

Before long, the kids were at the door, banging. Being a little "ticked," I hollered, "What do you want? This had better be important!"

Then Som exclaimed, "It's the most important thing in my life! The nipa hut's on fire!"

He was right. The palm leaf playhouse we bought for the kids was blazing, and the beautiful golden palm tree next to it was on fire. In five minutes, the nipa hut collapsed. Astonished neighbors were peeping over the low cement wall around our house. We grabbed the hose and doused the flames before they could leap to nearby trees.

Som had an explanation. He was playing with a magnifying glass that had caught the sun's rays that caused the fire. Much later we found that there was more to this story, but I'll leave it there.

What a privilege it was to marry Greg and Margaret with the U.S. Air Force Swordsmen present. The Swordsmen stood on both sides of the aisle, their swords forming an arch as the bride and groom marched in. In my office, twenty-five years later, I still have a large sword as remembrance of that occasion. These folks and a number of other Clarkites are still close friends today, and we keep in contact.

Now back to Bob. After pastoring at Clark for seven years, we felt a change was in order. For several weeks, we ministered in various countries, praying for God's leading. Then clearly, we were led to return back to Thailand where we had been some years before.

Before leaving the Clark area, I wanted to visit with Bob as often as possible. As I got to know him better, I had shared with him the destructive aspects of his business. I told him that he should ask himself the question, WWJD (What would Jesus do?)

Walking up to the Flying Machine for our last visit, I found the door locked and a sign saying "Out of business." Neighbors directed me to a new location two blocks away. The new building sported a sign that read "Beauty School." There had to be a story here, as I never scolded Bob about his lifestyle or his business.

Bob explained that day that he felt a Christian should not be in the bar and brothel business. Well, I wanted to tell him this from the first time I met him. But it was better that the Lord speak to him. So as God spoke to him, he closed the bar and opened a beauty school for the former prostitutes. The girls learned how to fix hair and to do manicures.

The proud owner confessed that there was a lot more money in the bar business. But he felt at peace that this was what Jesus would do. Not long afterward, Bob sold the business and returned to the USA.

Just a thought: sometimes we feel we must "speak up" and even condemn or preach to people who cuss, drink, do drugs, etc. We may feel it's our ministry or our duty to set them straight. But if they know we care about them, and we build a bridge of friendship, eventually Jesus will shine through our lives and speak to them.

33

THE CRASHING DOVE

A crashing dove—that's what the colored windows looked like in our new church. Initially, it was agreed that we would have a beautiful window depicting a soaring dove. But when the huge window was delivered, the dove was in a nose-dive. I just felt sick as nothing could be done about it now. That's when Heather explained that the dove was not crashing, it was descending. Suddenly, everyone cheered up. For truly the growth of the work at Clark was "sponsored by the Holy Spirit." The dove had descended upon us. We had faced and overcome many adventures and challenges during the church building program.

Clark Air Force Base, located 50 miles north of Manila, was kind of like home in many ways. Of the 10,000 men there, many had their families with them and even their American automobiles. Base housing was pretty nice—all units were air-conditioned. But the majority of the families lived off-base in somewhat second-class subdivisions around our church. What a difference from our last assignment in UTAPAO where there were no modern conveniences at all.

At UTAPAO, there had not even been a village. Garbage piles, bars, drug dens, prostitute shacks and stilted huts were the norm. Our center in Thailand, called The Vine, wasn't up to American standards, yet was far above anything locally available. But Clark, in the Philippines was like a slice of home, even if everything was somewhat second-class.

In the Philippines, the huge palm trees and the honking jeepneys fascinated Debbie and Som. The jeepneys were old World War II jeeps converted to crowded people-movers. They were gaudily decorated, and their horns worked a lot better than their brakes.

Our first Sunday as pastors of Clark Assembly of God was quite eventful. For one thing, we were told that the church was averaging over 100 people. But on our first Sunday, only 25 were present.

As the people left after worship service, one man commented, "Nice sermon, but we won't be back!" With his wife and two kids in tow, he spoke cordially enough. "We decided we'd stick it out until the new pastor arrived. So you're here, and we're leaving!" Yes, it was a downer. But in the next few weeks things even got worse. The attendance gradually went down to 15 people for Sunday morning worship. I felt like the country preacher who bragged, "This place is going down slower than anywhere I've ever been."

Prayer—desperate prayer—was in order. When we felt things couldn't get any worse, a young airman from the Vine in Thailand jumped over our gate and sauntered up the walk. Jim Baggett! Time after time his steady, godly presence encouraged us. Slowly the church began to grow. We had a good location on the main road near a major gate of the base. It was also a good location for local businesses. Unfortunately, the local prostitutes saw it as a potential for their business also. It was common for them to hide in the shadows and target the men coming into church. Yes, the devil does use various tactics to keep people out of church!

VALIUM CAT

Not long after we moved into the parsonage next to the church, a wild cat moved into a wood pile next to our bedroom. One morning, we heard little meows from the stack of wood where she had made her home. She had four little kittens. Heather and the kids desperately wanted them as pets. We already had a dog, and our house was constantly full of company, so cruel Dad said, "No!" But behind the scenes, Heather and the kids ganged up on me. Heather went to the vet and got four Valium tablets to tranquilize each of the kittens. They put the tranquilizers into balls of tuna fish and placed them inside the woodpile home. Good plan, right?

Unfortunately, the mother cat was not in on the plan. She gobbled down all four chunks of tuna and all four Valium tablets. Soon the momma cat was so spaced out she could barely drag herself around. But when we would get near her, she would jump and collapse just beyond our reach. After two days, she was almost back to normal. My rebellious family had somehow captured two of the wild kittens and brought them into the house. These cats were soon tamed. They did become real buddies for our children for the years ahead.

BEER GETS THE JOB DONE

The church had so many trees in front of it that it was hardly visible. Twice when I had newly arrived, I had passed right by the church while trying to find it. Something had to be done with at least one of those gigantic trees. I had a thing about churches having attractive signs and having no trees hiding the building.

Eventually, several men were hired to cut the tree. They soon gave up. "Too hard," they said, "the tree is too huge."

One day, I returned after being gone for several hours. To my astonishment, the largest of the trees had been cut down. The work crew was resting against a stump. "How did they get it done?" I inquired.

One of my helpers, who was not totally sanctified replied, "I just got them a case of San Miguel beer and they got it down. But they're a little drunk right now!" I was a bit shocked and embarassed and hoped that the congregation never discovered what incentives were used to accomplish this feat.

By God's grace and a committed core of people, the church continued to grow. When God begins to bless, we know the devil will show up. We didn't have long to wait.

ACCUSED OF STEALING-HOW NOT TO HANDLE CONFLICT

One Saturday night, I was in my study at the church, next to the parsonage. A very angry young navy man barged into the office. His face was red. "I found out, I've got you! You've been stealing from the church!" he shouted. I had no idea what Chuck (not his real name) was talking about. But he was waving a receipt for his giving to the church that had my name on it. He thought I personally got all the money he gave to the church.

I tried to explain that Americans that gave money to foreign organizations based overseas couldn't get IRS credit for it. So our missions department had suggested a paper transaction. All church donations were shown to flow in and out of our foreign missions account in Springfield, Missouri. But Chuck wasn't listening. He wanted an apology and blood. I tried to calm him down with logic, but it didn't work. So I decided to try a different method.

Chuck then showed me his receipt. For the entire year, he'd given only $400 total. The amount seemed rather small since he had an excellent rank and good salary. So I tried this other approach. "Chuck, with as much money as you're earning, you should be ashamed to complain about what happened to your $400!" Well, this didn't help. In fact, he got a lot madder.

I tried desperately to calm him down. Finally, I thought, as he was screaming and hollering at me, that I should just take the bull by the horns. Chuck was about six feet two inches tall and and weighed over 200 pounds. I was five feet ten and 140 pounds. In spite of this, I proceeded to take authority. "Chuck, I want you to sit down and shut your mouth right now!"

It was as if I had poured gas on the fire. He went totally berserk. First, he smashed my desk, and then he knocked over the bookcases. Then he broke the office chair, until all that was left was me hiding in the corner, praying. I was hoping maybe he had used up all of his energy destroying my office, and that God would somehow intervene. I'm thankful that he did not finish me off, but instead he just cussed me out thoroughly and left. As he stormed out the door, he yelled, "I'm going to a deacon's house and I'm going to come back and burn your a——."

Well anyhow, Sunday morning came, and the Lord was gracious to give us a good service. I knew that one of our deacons was a dear friend of Chuck's. So without telling the deacons about the problem, after the worship service I invited them for a little meeting in my office. I had left things as they were, totally destroyed. When they walked in, the men gasped and asked, "What happened here?" I told them about my Saturday night meeting with "Brother Chuck!"

Well, there was no more problem as far as they were concerned. The only unfortunate thing is that Chuck never came back to church. I'm sure there were better ways to handle this. In fact, I've heard over the years that when we come to church, we have two buckets in our hands. One is a bucket of water and one is a bucket of gas. If there's a problem or confusion, we can choose to throw on the water and put out the blaze, or throw on the gas and cause an explosion. Well, I think I did the wrong thing that time. However, looking back, I'm not sure how I could have satisfied the rage of "Brother Chuck."

TWO PIES WORTH $10,000

In just a few months at Clark, our chapel was full and it was time to start a building fund. Local banks were not very stable or trustworthy. But our mission's field treasurer in Manila had found a wonderful plan for investing our mission's money at a high yield. We, along with several other missionaries, invested our money through Brother Joe (not his real name) who managed it for us. Our church had given him a deposit of $10,000.

Several weeks went by, and it was time for our annual Philippine Assembly of God Field Fellowship meeting in Manila. We had about 60 missionaries on the field at that time. As I walked into the meeting room, there was a strange atmosphere of apprehension.

The first item on the agenda was a discussion of $50,000 missing from the mission's fund managed by Brother Joe. Somehow Joe had "misplaced" this rather large sum of money that was to be used for ministry in the Philippines.

The color drained from my face and I shook inside. I had given him all of our building fund money, the entire $10,000. I turned to Heather, "What can I do?"

Obviously, Joe chose not to attend the meeting. We had to act quickly. So I left the meeting, stopped by a local bakery, got two of Joe's favorite pies and dashed to his house. At first, it didn't appear he'd let me in. When he finally opened the door, all I could say was "Joe, I know that you're the treasurer and the books are messed up. And I don't know about all the money that's missing. But you do keep money hidden in the house. So tonight, before I leave, I need $10,000."

Can you believe, Joe left for a few moments and brought back a stack of bills, $10,000? I truly believe he was a good man who got sucked into investing missions money in a shaky business deal of some sort that went broke. When I got back to the meeting before it adjourned, I never mentioned to the other fellows about our money being returned to us. Unfortunately, we were the only missionaries to get any money out of the missing $50,000. (Since then, even tighter controls were put in place so that this would never happen again.)

BUILDING IN A THIRD WORLD COUNTRY

Choosing an architect and contractor in a third world country is tricky. Our architect had the best references. But all too soon, we discovered the references were exaggerated.

Fortunately for us, Heather's parents, Frank and Lillian Reed, had come out to visit us in the Philippines. Dad Reed was an outstanding Canadian architect. His specialty was designing churches and schools.

Our contractor began to dig footings for our new building, big ten-foot-deep holes. Then she (the architect/contractor was a lady) seemed confused. There were no rocks to build a foundation on. I'm no genius, but even I knew that the whole island was sand and the deeper you dug the more sand you would find.

Dad Reed came to the rescue. "Why not pour cement in the bottom of the holes?" he suggested. "Then put your foundation on top of the cement as if it were a solid rock." This problem cropped up during the very first week of construction. The eight-month project would drag on for another 14 months with near disasters popping up every few days.

During a building project in the Philippines, we found the custom was for the laborers to live on site. Some of our twenty men brought their wives and their kids with them. A few even included their dogs and radios. With our home and new building project all on one acre, things became pretty chaotic.

Then building materials started to disappear. So the iron rebar was stored on the tin roof over our bedroom. At sun-up for weeks, men trampled over our roof, screeching the iron across the corrugated tin.

One day, the architect came to me in my office. She said it was time for us to hire a structural engineer, as well as an electrical engineer. And then she confessed, "This is the largest building I've ever worked on. I'm not qualified to hire these engineers. You're going to have to interview them and hire them yourself." I sat totally astonished at what was facing me. I've had a few ideas about who the antichrist might be. But I had no clue whatever what was involved in hiring these two engineers. The church board was already nervous, so it wouldn't help to tell them of my dilemma. In fact, the church treasurer resigned the day we voted to start the construction.

THE POWER OF FRIENDSHIP AND PRAYER

Many late nights of prayer followed. I pored over plans that I really could not understand. Sometimes, I'd be in the church office at 11:00 or 12:00 p.m. More than once, as I was crying out to God, John Birkinbine and Lloyd Francis would walk into my office. These men were such a tremendous blessing. (I'm sad to say that I preached John's funeral just a few months ago, and his best buddy, Lloyd, also shared in the service.) These men often dropped by after working the late shift on the Air Force Base flight line. They were two of the youngest men on our church board.

"We don't know all you're struggling with, Pastor, but we just came by to say we love you and are praying for you." Numerous times, I've told these men that their prayers on those lonely and nerve-racking nights sustained me. Even though my understanding of the drawings was limited, the Lord enabled me to ask the engineers the proper questions. In the end, good men were hired and the work was done well.

MORE ABOUT THE DOVE WINDOW

One day a shocking letter arrived from the States. One of the young couples who were active at our church had returned to their home in New York state. Steve and Debbie Thimsen were so special. Debbie wrote that Steve had had a terrible motorcycle accident. Enroute to work, he was hit by a truck. We could not believe that Steve was dead.

Being overseas, you get very close to each other. There is no family nearby, you all become an extended family. When they first arrived, I had visited Steve and Debbie to invite them to church. He was a dog handler with the military police. They made a fresh commitment to the Lord, and both became leaders in the church.

One morning at sun-up, our doorbell rang. It was Steve and Debbie. Steve was all bent over in pain. Debbie said, "We're on our way to the base emergency room. Steve's back is killing him. But we decided we don't need to go to a hospital. We'll just go to the Burgess' house and he'll get healed!"

This young couple was not expecting a nice pious prayer. They were expecting a miracle! I was only half awake at sunrise and not up to any miracles. But boy, did Heather and I pray! God answered prayer immediately. Steve straightened up. A smile replaced the look of agony, and they went on their way rejoicing.

Now there was no rejoicing with this letter. Steve was gone; it still hurts today. We loved this couple deeply.

Then the shocker. After the details of Steve's wreck, Debbie had a surprise for us. She knew we were in the middle of building a new church. So she wanted information on how to send a tithe from Steve's life insurance policy to help with the project.

Immediately, I shot back a letter stating we would not accept any life insurance money. She had a little girl to care for and faced an uncertain financial future.

But Debbie was a determined young lady. In her fiery reply she said, "I'm so disappointed in you, Pastor Burgess. You taught us to trust the Lord, to put Him first and believe He would supply our needs. The Lord directed me to tithe on the life insurance, but you're blocking what God wants to do!"

Enclosed in her letter was a generous check. Now we began to think of some part of the new building which would be a tribute to Steve's memory. A large stained glass window could be seen by hundreds of people that passed by the building daily, so that's how the dove window was conceived.

GOD ARRESTED A POLICEMAN

The ministry of the church at Clark touched many men, women and couples. One day, while I was driving on the base, I saw blue flashing lights. A motorcycle policeman signaled me to pull over. Yes, he was really after me. I think I must have made an illegal turn.

As I got out of the car, the helmeted policeman approached me. He stopped, and exclaimed, "Oh I'm sorry Pastor Burgess, I didn't know it was you."

"Well, Richard," I replied, "I must have done something wrong. You were just doing your job."

Richard and his wife, Auring Versolinka, had been in the church a few days earlier. He had not attended church much in recent years. Richard was a very bitter preacher's son, mad at God for his dad's death. Their family lived in Oregon.

Richard's father had been a dedicated pastor. When a flood devastated their area, his dad took a plane up so church members could survey their property and determine when they might return home safely. Usually Richard went along on these jaunts. But on one final flight, he stayed behind. There was a crash, and his beloved dad was killed. Richard couldn't understand how God could let a man die while doing His work.

At the altar that Sunday, Richard poured out his heart. He told me, "I'm the president of the Philippine National Motorcycle Racers Club, and we race on Sundays. If I give my heart to God, will I have to give up racing and come to church on Sunday?" I declined to answer and told him he'd have to do what he felt pleased the Lord.

Later, I found out it was a setup. Richard thought I'd tell him to forget Sunday racing events. Then he would be justified in quitting church for good. The fact that I did not answer made him mad. Well, this was about the time he stopped me for the illegal turn. A few days later, a beaming Richard was in church again. He had offered his resignation to the racing club, saying that he had to be in church on Sunday. But he was so respected as a great guy and champion racer, the club changed their racing days from Sunday to Saturday. God had arrested a policeman. The Versolinkas' later returned to the U.S.A and are still serving the Lord today!

TYPHOON

Typhoons hit the tropics every year. A few lash an area at only 60 miles an hour. But winds over 100 miles an hour are quite common. One typhoon we encountered was a true adventure. Our yardman rushed to knock down all the coconuts from the palm trees surrounding our house. He explained that a 100-mile-an-hour wind would send a coconut through a concrete wall.

In Tennessee, tornadoes come and last maybe five or ten minutes. But a typhoon may last six or eight hours! First comes the wind, then very heavy, blinding rain, followed usually by flooding. Then after three to four hours, all becomes calm. The storm seems to be over. But we were told to watch out for the "eye of the storm." In the core, or "eye," the typhoon is calm for about 30 minutes. Then the storm returns with a vengeance. Often, inexperienced folks are caught unaware and lose their lives when they venture out into the "eye." Usually flying coconuts and debris cause many injuries.

A typhoon was headed straight for Clark. The whole family was marshalled to hurriedly tape plastic over our louvered windows. When the radio reported that winds of 185 miles an hour were headed toward us, it sounded pretty bad. We realized that plastic on the windows wasn't important. Wind that high would knock the entire house flat.

But what about the church? The walls were still going up, and were not well supported at this time. The building underway had required so much sacrifice by so many. Now all seemed hopeless in the face of a killer typhoon.

Quick action was required. We stopped taping windows and went to our knees in prayer. Jesus had calmed the storms on the Sea of Galilee, and we needed this storm calmed.

Our anxiety rose as the time for the typhoon to hit came, and then passed. There was some rain but no high wind. The next day, we found the typhoon had changed course and gone north of us into a sparsely populated area. It did very little damage, with no loss of life. The Lord had been merciful once again.

COSTLY LOAN

Building programs are costly, and can be full of unpleasant surprises, especially if you are working outside the U.S.A. Yet the servicemen and their families were excited as the building project began. Many gave sacrificially. This amazed us, because a large number who gave would not be around for the completion of the project. Our church had an "organized split" about every year-and-a-half. This was the average time people were with us before their tours were completed and they returned back to the States.

The greatest help came from those employed by the Department of Defense (DOD) as schoolteachers for the children of the military. Our church was blessed with four such people. Margaret Veary and Cecelia Ward had been anchors in the early days when Henry Culbreth pastored the church. They were so encouraging. Often they would loan us their air-conditioned apartment where we could "veg out" on our day off.

The other couple was Leon and Sandra Parsley. This energetic couple not only earned their Master's degrees, as did Margaret and Cecelia, but also attained their PhD degrees while in the Philippines. Sandra was a tremendous help as the treasurer for the building project.

Leon had drifted from his Assembly of God roots when he met Sandra, who was a very devout Roman Catholic. He did faithfully attend mass as he promised. But they started coming to our church after mass each Sunday, mainly through their friendship with Margaret and Cecelia. It's amazing that most people come to church and stay because of friendships.

So many gave sacrificially and more than I was ever comfortable with. One Filipina house girl (maid) brought her two-ounce solid gold chain valued at $700 for the building. Many Orientals put their savings into gold, which they feel is safer than putting money in the bank. This girl made only $35 a week. So she gave the equivalent of nearly two years' total income! Like Debbie Thimsen, the young house girl lectured me when I was hesitant to receive her gold chain. I just don't ever like to take advantage of people. I want them to give, not out of pressure, but out of the leading of the Spirit. Sometimes I've been rebuked because of turning down people's offerings.

For weeks, we had prayed about what we personally should give. No cash was available, but we had accrued equity in a home in Memphis. We secured a loan on the home and put it into the new building. Sometimes it's good to put everything on the altar before God. We thought surely we would lose the house, as there was no obvious way to ever repay the loan. But through generous supporters a year later, we were able to repay the lien against our house. It was kind of like Abraham placing his son Isaac on the altar. God gave him back to Abraham. We put our house on the altar, and the Lord gave it back to us. He must have said something like, "I see that you really love Me and trust Me, so I'm going to give it back to you."

COMPLETE AT LAST

Finally, the work was finished—a beautiful, fan-shaped sanctuary to accommodate 300, with central air-conditioning. This center of evangelism had to be up to U.S.A. standards because most of our people were American military.

Cecil Blackwood brought the quartet and a tour group all the way from Memphis to Manila. He also brought and donated a very fine Bose PA system. The Blackwood Brothers were the first ones to break in the new sound system.

One minor problem remained. I promised the church that 80% of the building loan would be repaid before we left on our normal furlough back to the States. By the time of the completion, all funds were exhausted. It was important that the promise be kept. But how? Together, Heather and I decided I would stay behind in the Philippines and she and the children would return to Memphis. Then she could get the children in school and possibly contact supporters and bail me out.

ALONE!

Putting Heather, Debbie and Som on the plane in Manila was tough. Tough because there was no way to determine how long I would need to remain at Clark until the necessary monies were received. I believe my tears were successfully hidden until they boarded the flight.

This major project in a third world country had left me drained physically, emotionally and maybe spiritually. It was a lonely drive, the two hours from Manila back to Clark. I was near total collapse.

Really, I did not know how close to the edge I was. An outstanding missionary couple, the Nultemeiers, were assigned to replace us during our one-year furlough in the States. A year later, after we had furloughed and returned to Clark, I asked someone about this missionary couple. I said, "I know of these folks' excellent reputation. I'm just sorry I never met them personally."

One of the board members stared at me in amazement. "Pastor, don't you remember that I took you to the Manila Airport to meet them last year?" He continued, "They lived in the parsonage with you for two weeks!" The stress had been so great, my mind had totally shut down.

Several Memphis friends who had generously supported our ministry in the past, responded to Heather's appeal. Unexpectedly, funds came from other sources also. The Christian allergist who had given me 120 shots in my back a few months earlier had told me that he would be willing to help us at some point. So I told Heather to ask this doctor to consider a $1,000 loan for the building. When Heather went to visit him, he took out his checkbook and wrote $3,000. When Heather replied we weren't sure we could repay that much, he pointed to the bottom of the check. It was marked GIFT! Thus, after my being stranded for four weeks, all the remaining bills were paid.

What a relief to board the flight for the good ole U.S.A. As the plane lifted off over Manila, the rice fields and the tiny islands faded away and ahead stretched 12 hours of flight over the blue Pacific. Four years had passed. The Lord had been merciful to us during our tour in the Philippines. Again we realized that whatever good was done, it was "sponsored by the Holy Spirit."

34

SHE SAW A SNAKE ATTACKING

After serving in the Philippines for a total of nearly seven years, we transferred back to Thailand for two years. Our missionary force there had been depleted by illness and furloughs. Instead of being in remote UTAPAO, we located now in the bustling, mega metropolis of Bangkok.

On our earlier missionary assignment, we had been with the American military in Thailand. Now we would work exclusively with our Thailand national church. This meant I would have to learn the terribly difficult Thai language. Thai is somewhat like Chinese, with five different tones. The same word can mean five different things, depending on the tone. It's very easy to get yourself into trouble!

The language school became my second home. Then while driving in the car, the family was tortured as I listened to the Thai language and my taped attempt to speak it. After two years of painful study, I progressed to be able to conduct mission business by telephone—no hand signals could help here!

Interspersed with language school, I was also the acting Field Chairman attempting to coordinate the work of our other missionaries. Then I had still another briefcase in my trunk with notes for the Bible school classes that I taught. Also, I served as the Dean of Education for our Bangkok Theological Center. So there was a fourth briefcase with notes for planning Bible courses and schedules.

About this time, Jimmy Swaggart faced some drastic charges, and he had to cut all missionary projects. He had been one of our major supporters. Our finances took a nosedive. There was no choice for us but to move to more cramped, poorly located housing.

About every six months, with heavy rains and an incoming tide, our new apartment got three or four feet of water in the yard. Our third floor unit was rather safe from the flooding, but the ground floor occupants had to be evacuated by boat. And in the parking lot, water crept up over the fenders of our poor Speed-the-Light car on two occasions. It was a challenge to sit in water, driving our vehicle, while a young Thai boy held the hood up to prevent the radiator fan from flooding out the engine.

A stroll down our soi (Thai for street) was interesting. We lived across from the police station, which was next to one of the largest brothels in the region. In recent years, such brothels have been responsible for the epidemic spread of AIDS in Thailand. Next to the police station, were piles of wrecked automobiles. If wrecks were brought in the night before, we learned not to look in the windows too closely. Sometimes body parts from victims may not yet have been removed!

One day we were arranging some furniture in our apartment. As I was moving things around, I spied an electrical cord under a table. For some reason, I cautiously picked it up, not realizing it was a live, 220-volt wire. As I picked up the shielded portion, the end of the wire bent somehow, and latched onto my left hand. In the tropical heat I was soaked with perspiration, so I was thoroughly grounded.

As the power shook my body, I attempted to pull the wire from my left hand with my right. I was convulsing and could not get it loose. I screamed for Heather who was resting in the bedroom. But the pain and panic of the moment was such that my screams were probably not very loud. Also, the air-conditioning was running in the bedroom. My heart was pounding almost out of my chest. I cried out to God. The next thing I knew, I was lying on the floor with the hot wire there beside me.

The current burned two deep gashes down to the bone of my left hand. The power had actually cooked the flesh, and it took months to heal. Years later, I still have the two-pronged scar. Every time I notice the scars, I remember God's grace and mercy to me!

Not long after this frightening event, I heard from my precious Aunt Nell Brewer. Actually, she wasn't a relative, but a dear, dear friend to our family. Aunt Nell told me of a dream. "Gene, in a dream I saw you there in your house on the mission field. An ugly snake grabbed your hand and would not turn loose. It looked like it was going to kill you. I awoke and began to pray for God to deliver you. And as I kept praying, I finally felt peace. (The old timers called this 'praying through.') Do you know what this could mean?" she asked.

I was dumbfounded. "Well," I explained, "it wasn't really a snake, but a hot electrical wire that caught me and almost electrocuted me. I believe that the time you prayed was exactly the same time the current released me and my life was spared."

On two occasions, friends who were in touch with God had dreams or visions of my distress. Often, I've wondered what would have happened to me if they hadn't awakened to pray. So, as you pray before sleeping tonight, why not ask the Lord to wake you if someone is in a crisis?

35

"THERE'S LIFE IN JESUS' NAME"

The Bangkok to Pattaya Road was crowded as usual. I had been ministering at our church in Pattaya on Sunday. Now I had a two-hour drive back to Bangkok in heavy traffic.

Ahead of me was a large, overloaded truck. The freight seemed to be bouncing—apparently some huge metal containers were not anchored securely. I wondered what would happen to me if one of those containers flew off onto the roof of my car. I didn't have long to wonder.

It was always a delight to preach in Pattaya. There, luxury resorts and fine hotels lined the beaches. Sadly, it also teemed with infamous bars and brothels. Here in the midst of sin city, we'd had a part in planting a vibrant, dynamic, growing church.

The church had been born out of our English Language School at UTAPAO. In those days, midway through the evening classes taught by young airmen, Pastor Preecha would minister God's Word. Many of the Thai Buddhist students were saved and accepted public baptism in the Gulf of Siam. The new believers were very committed, and together started a new church. They brought their friends, studied their Bibles and began to tithe to the work until it was self-supporting.

Often at UTAPAO, we prayed that God would close the bars and the brothels that were around the base. These were common around every base in Southeast Asia. When the Vietnam War was over, many new believers moved up the beach to Pattaya, 40 miles north to find jobs and pioneer a second church. The church at UTAPAO continued to thrive. Today, if you could visit this area, you would find a fine church, and also you'd find every bar and brothel around the former American base closed.

The Thai Christians who went to Pattaya found jobs in the booming tourist industry. They served as chefs, waitresses, maids, etc. Once we had a large reunion with those who worked at the plush Regent Hotel—all had been saved at the Vine or at the English Language School. These friends, with the assistance of Pastor Preecha, wanted to start a new church. They appealed to missionary Bruce Mumm and myself to help buy property. We had some personal funds to commit and found a suitable spot 50 yards from the main road. They later moved to a better location, and today have a lovely, flourishing church.

Some from the UTAPAO area even went north of Pattaya to Thonburi, where they found good jobs in the natural gas industry. Again, a self-supporting church was established there.

Thus, every time I went back to this area where it all started, it was with a great sense of pride. Pride in what the Lord had done. Three thriving churches!

On the drive back from Pattaya that afternoon, I was just praising the Lord for His mercy. And I was watching the truck in front of me. It happened in a nano second. The truck hit a bump, and a huge steel container came hurtling right toward my windshield. At that moment I was listening to a tape from First Assembly in Memphis. It was playing the song, "There's Life in Jesus' Name!" There was nothing I could do but cry out, "Jesus," as I saw the container rushing at me. It seemed to nose dive, however, and skid towards the edge of the highway. I only hit it a glancing blow with the bumper of the car. The full story was later published in our *Pentecostal Evangel.* The bumper was dented but once again, God was merciful and spared my life.

Most people don't realize the greatest danger that missionaries face is not disease, robbery or even terrorism. The greatest hazards are on third world highways. Driving, especially at night, is dangerous in any third world country.

Because of several very close calls, I basically have refused to get out on the highway at night. But a few days after the truck incident, necessity put a team of us on the highway on a dark, rainy night.

Our mission had asked us to deliver Bibles and supplies to the Cambodian Refugee Camp on the Thai border. The poor souls living there were fleeing the murderous Pol Pot. He was responsible for the deaths of over one million of his countrymen. The refugees lived in hopeless conditions in rows of grass huts.

On our arrival at the camp, a crowd rushed toward us to sell the crudest of handicrafts. Others were clutching handfuls of Cambodian currency—now totally worthless. All their savings was in a currency that was no longer legal.

We delivered a great portion of our goods to Thai soldiers to distribute to the destitute in this dangerous area where there were frequent attacks by communist rebels. One of the short-term missionaries tried to speak to the commander in English. Then the missionary insulted the Thai commander for not replying to him in English. It was embarrassing to be in this missionary's company. So in my limited Thai, I explained to the officer that this American was an idiot and suggested he ignore him!

That incident later prompted me, as the acting field chairman, to insist on Thai language study for each missionary. If anyone was to be in the country for at least six months, I felt he should know enough Thai to communicate with the local people on a basic level. Furthermore, I felt that if people couldn't commit to at least learning to communicate to some degree, they should not stay. This position made me very unpopular with several folks who could not even ask where the bathroom was after being in the country for two years. This language problem usually develops when good folks come out for short terms and then extend. By then they have become so deeply involved in ministry, they have no time to go to language school. Many think that language study is not necessary if they have interpreters.

Finally, we were on our way back to Bangkok. There was no choice but to drive at night. There were no hotels in this remote region. And we thought, *Well we're only three hours from the city.* Soon we'd be home with no problem—well not much problem.

Dan Grubbs was an excellent missionary and driver. Another missionary and I were to assist as lookouts for trouble in the downpour at night. Suddenly, Dan slammed on the brakes and exclaimed, "I think I hit something or someone!" There was a bump, but the road was rough. We decided we had better investigate!

So the three of us walked along the roadside calling out in case we had hit somebody. Then we heard a groan down in the muddy rice paddy. Our flashlight beam reached a man lying in the mud. He was alive and struggling to get up. We helped him up to the roadway. He was dazed but did not seem seriously hurt.

Then the shocker. He said he had a friend with him. So now, quite concerned, we looked in all directions for the other man we had apparently also hit. We heard another groan. Sure enough, the other guy was regaining consciousness down in the muddy rice paddy. He also was not hurt seriously.

Apparently, both men, both very drunk, were riding down the middle of the highway in their black Thai farmers' outfits on black bicycles. It's incredible—their bikes were smashed and their clothing torn, but aside from a few minor cuts, they were lucid and walking.

Now relieved that they were okay, we next worried about the Thai army patrols. If they saw the men and heard about the collision, they would put us Americans in jail. So quickly, we pooled our cash to pay for both bikes, new clothes and a bit extra for any medicines, and got moving in a hurry.

Several missionary friends of ours have been involved in accidents overseas. Usually they were taken to jail and not even allowed to contact their families for days. So we were grateful to God for His mercy once again.

Through no merit of our own, this trip to the refugee camp had been "sponsored by the Holy Spirit."

36

UNCLE BILL GOT HIS MONEY!

Each night our children, Debbie and Som, would pray, "Dear God, please help Uncle Bill to get his money." At some point we were able to assure them that Uncle Bill had gotten lots of money. But since they loved Bill so much, we omitted some of the details of Bill's mysterious prosperity.

Among Bill's numerous talents was lock-picking. This came in handy the day that we met him. Our servicemen's center, The Vine, moved from cramped quarters next to the bars. Our new home was a little more peaceful—no bars, only brothels nearby!

By faith, I had rented two large buildings and had them converted into five apartments. One apartment was for our Thai co-worker's family, and one was for ourselves. Military men leased the remaining three apartments with their wives. The rent on those three apartments paid for the whole project. This way, the church income could be focused on outreach.

Frustration greeted us on our moving day into the new Vine. The workmen had inadvertently locked our bedroom door. That's when Uncle Bill offered his talent. In ten seconds, he picked the door lock and we began to move in!

Bill, Norm (the sweet potato man), and several other retired G.I.s made our rec room downstairs their second home. They, along with active duty Air Force men, joined us for two free, home cooked meals daily.

Unfortunately, Bill was always broke. But he was always expecting some big checks from the U.S.A. He was a mysterious fellow. I suspected he and some of his other buddies were wanted back in the States. At any rate, they stayed on in Thailand working angles to get a few dollars.

With scores of men coming for meals, we had two house girls, or maids, who cooked and cleaned. They also were suspicious of Bill.

Time arrived for our periodic visa trip to Bangkok, three hours north. These trips were always tense. There were anxious waits at the immigration office to seek another three-month extension of our visas. (For a $5,000 bribe you could get a permanent visa. The Japanese were the only ones who could afford such).

When we returned from Bangkok, I tried to find my camera, but it was missing. Then I couldn't locate the tape recorder—it was missing. Next the big shock, all of Heather's jewelry was gone. Everything we had of any value was stolen. But we had securely double-locked our bedroom door. Bill?

Yes, he'd been around a lot, but no one had seen him go upstairs to our own quarters. Bill and his "girlfriend" didn't come around for a while after our return, though.

A couple of days later, a Thai lady told us Bill had sold a nice ruby ring cheap to one of her friends. This was the ring for which we had scraped together money to celebrate the birth of our son, Som. Rumors of the other stolen things gradually filtered through to us.

I went to the Thai police for help. They gave me some unique advice. "You go and catch this guy and bring him to us and we'll question him!" Now Bill was 6'2", weighing over 200 lbs., and I was 5'10", and only weighed 140 lbs. I could just picture me dragging this guy down the street. Fortunately, our insurance replaced most of the lost articles.

Things returned to normal, and three months passed before Bill showed up again. His first words were shockers. He blurted, "Pastor Burgess, I had to come and forgive you for saying you thought I had stolen things from you!"

"No, Bill," I replied, "I didn't tell people I thought you stole our things. I told them I knew you stole them!"

Then the ultimate con—"My new Thai wife wants to be a Christian. In fact, she wants to be baptized and have our baby dedicated. I don't want to come here, but I have to bring them." Soon the three of them showed up for church and the free meals. But everybody watched Bill like a hawk.

Unfortunately, word came again from the Thai police that our visas could not be extended. Now we'd have to make another trip out of the country for new permits.

On our last trip for visas we had gone to Saigon. It was 1971; the Vietnam War was at its height in violence. In Saigon, every street corner seemed fortified with tanks and machine gun emplacements.

So seeking a safer place, this time we chose Laos. Our plane landed on the Thai-Laotian border. From there, we boarded a rickety, wooden boat to cross the Mekong River. A "taxi" took us on the 60-mile trip up to the capital of Vientiane. Along the way we were stopped and advised where the communist guerillas were fighting. Vientiane was filled with communist spies, CIA agents, Laotian troops, communist sympathizers, etc. We began to wonder if Saigon might have been safer!

After two days, our mission was accomplished, and with visas in hand we made the long trip back to Bangkok and on to UTAPAO. We were confident that our two helpers would give our kids loving care. There was no worry about theft. Everybody was watching Uncle Bill, even though he was now newly "converted."

Before leaving the Vine on this trip, Heather had one of her great ideas. We found a bomb fuse box with a hinged lid, and covered it with beautiful blue Thai silk. The top formed a nice seat, like a stool. Neatly hidden under a ruffle were two heavy-duty locks. We could keep all of our valuables safe in the box. Heather did keep out the ruby ring we'd replaced, and stuffed it in a shoe in the closet.

After returning and spending some good times with the kids, we turned in. Before going to sleep, we checked the box of valuables. Opening our homemade safe, we stared in disbelief—empty! We were speechless. How could anyone get through two new locks on our door and even find the safe, plus pick the two locks? Only one person had such "gifts"—Bill. Even though our staff tried to watch him, Bill was no ordinary thief. Coincidently, Bill never returned to the servicemen's church or center again.

But our kids couldn't forget him. He had spent time with them and played with them. So for many months at bedtime prayers, they would remind us, "Now let's pray Uncle Bill will get his money!" As they really loved him, not until adulthood did we tell them how Uncle Bill got some of his money. It's good to know that God keeps the records. If we give even a cup of cold water in His name, or a few possessions, He rewards us.

After ministering in the Philippines for seven years, we returned to Thailand. This time we lived in Bangkok and worked with our national church. Several times we went down near UTAPAO to the resort city of Pattaya for ministry. Twice I spotted Bill. For some time, I watched him at a distance. He was hustling tourists into shops where he would get a kickback. Bill was now thin, emaciated, chain-smoking and looking much older.

Since Bill was a well-known character in Pattaya, periodic news would reach us through Thai Christians who had known him back in UTAPAO. Later, someone told us they thought he had been killed, but there were no details.

After our return to the USA from Thailand, Bill's mother somehow located us. She was concerned about her son. I gave her all the positive news I could think of. There seemed to be no point in telling her of the thefts, or of the rumors of his death.

Literally hundreds of men found Christ in Thailand and returned to live productive lives. But unfortunately, there were some like Bill who made a series of wrong choices. Someone has said that we are a product of our choices. We make the choices and the choices determine what we become.

37

I HAD JUDGE HOOKS ARRESTED—A CONFESSION

Yes, the title is true. I'm certainly not proud of it. But it's a part of my history.

Benjamin Hooks, in my opinion, is one of the most outstanding men in America today. Without question, he is a stellar black leader in the country. He's one of those great men who are "colorblind." He was generous enough to forgive me for my poor judgment.

The September 10, 2003 *Commercial Appeal* carried a huge article on Hooks. The writer, Fredric Koeppel, mentioned some of his accomplishments. These accomplishments included his appointment as Shelby County Criminal Court Judge in 1966, the first black judge in the South since Reconstruction. Later, he was appointed by President Richard Nixon to the Federal Communications Commission in 1972 where he served until he was elected to lead the NAACP from 1977 to 1992.

The things I write in this chapter may sound strange in 2004. Today, most churches are reaching out to minorities, especially black families. Yet for the most part, they aren't coming. But back in the early 1960's, we attempted to keep the black folks out of our churches. What a paradox!

Segregation had many ugly facets. For the black man, it meant inequality. For the white man, integration was a threat. Ben Hooks was a firebrand crusader in Memphis for total integration. This included integration not only of our schools and restaurants, but also places of worship.

Looking back 40 years, the black man's struggle for integration was certainly a just cause. It was long past due. But unfortunately, this issue was not always handled with reason. The southern whites felt politicians were simply aiding blacks to get their votes. Yes, there was plenty of fear and bigotry. Many whites felt that integration was proper. Yet they felt change was being pushed too fast. Of course, it was 200 years late.

Well, back to the arrest. In early 1960, I served as a youth coordinator for our Memphis Assembly of God churches. A large youth rally was planned for the outdoor Overton Park Shell. It was my responsibility to serve as the head usher.

The meeting started smoothly about 7:00 p.m. From my post in the rear of the gathering, I noted the arrival of three yellow school buses. It was about 7:30 p.m. A delegation of black teens and young adults clambered off the buses. My instructions were to seat any late arrivals in the rear of the band shell.

As the delegation arrived, I showed them to the rear seats since the service was already in progress. Yet the entire group pushed past me and dispersed themselves from the very front to every area of the arena. It was obvious from their demeanor they had not come to worship. At this particular time, not a single black person attended any of the Assemblies of God churches in Memphis.

The movement of so many into the service while it was in progress was disruptive. The presbyter for the Memphis area instructed me to call the police. It was a fiasco! Soon, the police moved through the crowd arresting the demonstrators. It was evident the delegation had come to make a statement. Their leader was a charismatic young black lawyer by the name of Benjamin Hooks. Hooks was charged with disturbing a religious worship service.

This episode sounds bizarre today. But 40 years ago, a lot of unpleasant events marred race relations. For this, we whites must shoulder much of the responsibility. Yes, I felt very embarrassed to face a fellow Christian, Ben Hooks, in court. Surely there must have been a better way for us to settle our disagreements. As far as the law was concerned, Hooks and his followers were guilty. As far as God was concerned, I was the guilty one. Through the years I've read often of Ben Hooks as he rose to national fame. And the more I read about him, the more petty I have felt.

Fast forward 40 years. As a member of the Memphis Ministerial Association, I try to attend most meetings. Usually a lunch is served. It helps inspire the pastors' attendance. I noticed a striking figure sitting at a table near me one day,. It was Benjamin Hooks. I had not seen him since the day we faced each other in court.

Today, he is the honored pastor of the Greater Middle Baptist Church in Memphis. Pastor Hooks' church hosted this particular meeting. As I looked at his kind face, the events at the Overton Park Shell replayed in my mind. I knew Pastor Hooks did not know me. But I felt he was due an apology, even if it was 40 years late.

Leaning across the table, I almost whispered, "I owe you an apology."

Pastor Hooks inquired, "Why do you think you owe me an apology?" Hooks is not only a great leader, but also a humble, compassionate, kind person.

Then I blurted out, "Do you remember leading a group in the Overton Park Shell in 1960? I was the guy that called the police and had you arrested. Please forgive me!"

As tears trickled down my cheeks, his eyes became misty. We embraced. It felt so good! It made me wish I had earlier remembered the scripture that says, "How good and pleasant it is when brothers live together in unity!" (Psalm 133:1 NIV)

38

GOD'S HIT MEN

In every church there are key individuals—respected leaders and people of influence. Whether elected formally or not, over time these folks become the ones you
can always count on. Usually they are faithful in their attendance. They are generous in their tithes and offerings. And usually they "pull their weight" in carrying out the work of the Lord. Most of these dedicated individuals have been in
the church longer than the pastor. Some may have survived two or three or more
pastors. They are rock solid. As a rule, nothing sways them.

Thank God for those whom the Bible describes as "unshakable." If the roof
blew off the church Saturday night, they'd be in their places Sunday morning
after helping replace the roof. The church couldn't survive without them. If the
preacher runs off with the secretary, they'll hang on and seek to keep the flock
together. Every church needs them to remain stable when the storms of adversity
blow.

In churches with a long history, strong leaders and their families may have
held key positions for 20 to 30 years or more. In smaller churches, their voices
and opinions are often valued more than those of the pastor. In such cases, their
influence easily becomes a two-edged sword.

Speaking of swords, that reminds me of poor old Malchus. Malchus was a
good man who was just doing his job. He was with the "raiding party" that
accosted Jesus in the Garden on that Good Friday evening. When Simon Peter
smelled trouble, he felt it was time to take charge. Something had to be done as
armed men surrounded the Lord. Being always quick to speak and act, Peter
drew his sword and swung. He possibly was aiming at someone's head, but anyhow, Malchus was the victim. He lost an ear rather than his head. No doubt
Peter felt pride in having done the "right thing" in defending the Lord. In current
mob terminology, he was "God's hit man." At a crucial moment he felt he knew
better than Jesus what should be done. His intentions were good as he attempted

to help Jesus out. But rather than thanks, Peter received a stern rebuke from our Lord.

Every church has good people like Peter. They sincerely strive to assist the church. Someone has said that key individuals come to church with two buckets in their hands. In one bucket is water and in the other is gasoline. If there is a problem or a hint of trouble, they feel it is vital to respond. And if the pastor is thought to be failing in some of his duties, they are the ones to be alerted. If they hear a complaint, they may simply use their bucket of water to extinguish a flame while it is small, or they may use the bucket of gasoline. In that case, suddenly something trivial becomes a blaze or a destructive explosion.

This chapter is not intended to hurt or defame. Nor is it intended to vindicate the writer. Hopefully, no one will feel we've endured near martyrdom! This chapter is dedicated to committed pastors and leaders. Eventually something mentioned here will seem strangely familiar to many.

Certainly, no one should think pastors are perfect. One of my sayings is, "Pastors are borderline human!" The pastor who is insensitive and dictatorial will cause much harm. "My way or the highway" hardly models the caring shepherd of Scripture. But if the leaders treat the pastor with disrespect, eventually the church will be hurt. One deacon shouted at a pastor in a business meeting, "I was here before you came, and I'll be here when you're gone!" When individuals, for whatever "good reasons" overreact, they become "God's hit men."

Unfortunately this syndrome is contagious. Children who watch their parents "nail" a pastor usually grow up thinking that is normal. That's why some congregations have earned the tag, "troubled churches" or "preacher killers." Unfortunately, these churches go through pastors every two to four years. Just about the time a church recovers from one sad disruption, another series of events brings another resignation.

Many in the congregation never figure out why pastors leave. Often the pastor who may have been hurt deeply in a private business meeting, says nothing. He brushes back the tears and says, "The Lord is leading us to go." The pain for the pastor's wife and kids may never completely heal. Unfortunately, the Lord has little to do with many resignations. Sometimes I joke that the U-Haul ™ trailer appearing in the front yard and the map to Alaska tipped him off to God's will.

A CHANGE IN MINISTRY

After completing 14 years as overseas missionaries, we sensed God was changing our direction. Before settling down to pastor in the States, I gave an entire year to travel across America to thank our supporting churches scattered in 16 states.

I did not tell the churches about our future plans to pastor until one Sunday, my son let the news out. A pastor took us to lunch after church. In conversation he commented, "I guess you can't wait to get back to Thailand?"

Usually quiet, Som blurted out, "We aren't goin' back!"

North To Canada: Vancouver, B.C.

A church in Canada invited us to come for an interview. As we flew up to visit, we discussed reimbursing the church for the "vacation." The snow-capped Rocky Mountains near Vancouver were breath-taking, but moving there to pastor seemed unlikely. This church was listed as one of the "16 Great Churches of the Assemblies of God of Canada."

Our interview with the board went smoothly. They assured us that although there were problems in the past, the church was just looking for the right man to lead them. Unfortunately the church had dropped down to 250 from about 500. But we were told the church was still very stable. They had an attractive, well-located building with a sanctuary seating 600. Adjoining the church was a lovely senior citizen's complex with 16 apartments. There was also a small church school, which we were told made money for the church. Most church schools tend to drain the church's assets, and at times it becomes the "tail that wags the dog." Could this school be different?

Someone told me years ago, "Be careful of the man who meets you at the airport, because generally that man will feel that you should follow all of his suggestions." Perhaps I should have been suspicious when he told us the type of car we should drive and the proper home to buy—both conservative. At any rate, we received 90% of the vote. And we accepted the invitation to be their pastor.

On our arrival we discovered several things. One, the church was $40,000 behind on current bills. Some parents were paying their kids' school bills into the regular offerings, often instead of paying tithes, to receive tax benefits. We also found that a core of influential people had practically killed the last pastor. He had led the church in three major building programs, and the church had grown from 200 to over 500. Yet some felt another pastor could do better. (This type of attitude has caused much pain in the Kingdom of God.) Also, a few key deacons wanted all staff members fired. I declined to dismiss them as there was no reason to do so. During the change of pastors, the staff had had no job descriptions and didn't know what was expected of them. All they needed was some direction.

"A lot of people in the church don't like you!" When I met a deacon for lunch one day, those were the first words out of his mouth. Guess what? This was the deacon who had met us at the airport on our initial visit. "Yes, a lot of people don't like you, but I can count them on one hand."

"Praise the Lord," I exclaimed. For by now the church had rebounded and grown to about 600. A mere handful of negative people did not sound like a problem.

The outspoken gentlemen mentioned above was a multi-millionaire, a friend of the Prime Minister, and was used to calling the shots in the church. Yet he was a good man in many ways. It's hard for wealthy, influential people to keep their controlling instinct in check. They simply feel they know what's best.

Since I did not cater to him in our board meetings, he eventually resigned. As strange as it may seem, even though he no longer served on the deacon board, the men would make no major decision without first consulting Brother George.*

Things got sticky when I requested a full audit of the church books. As I suspected, the church school was not even paying its own way. In fact, the church deficit of $40,000 was nearly identical to the deficit in the school's books!

As far as the congregation was concerned, the Lord was blessing and things were going smoothly. Yet the pressures on me from a core of men grew in intensity. It was hard to imagine that in spite of the tremendous progress the church was making, a small group of people sought to get people "on their side," and began demanding a vote of confidence for the pastor. One Sunday night after church, the ulcer-like pain I'd had ten years earlier returned. In the wee hours of the morning I struggled out of bed.

The next thing I remember was lying on the floor bathed in blood. Being so weak, I groaned to wake Heather. She sat up, saw me, and fainted!

Before long she revived and called for an ambulance. After three pints of blood and three days in the hospital, I was Okay. This was how "God spoke to me" to say farewell to the church. We still have very dear friends in the church today and have returned to preach there. Yes, Brother George still thinks he was doing God's work in encouraging us to leave. And yes, I still think highly of him.

*Name Change

Back To The Deep South: Jackson, Mississippi

Our next invitation came from a church in central Mississippi. Two of their key men drove nearly 3,000 miles to Canada in a huge U-Haul truck to get our furniture. One was a board member who became a very dear friend. He later admitted that he was one of the 15% who voted against our coming to the church. So he joked that God punished him by making him drive 6,000 miles round trip to move our furniture!

This church was located in the state capital. Through an annual Civic Appreciation Day, the Lord opened many doors to us. The State Attorney General, Lieutenant Governor, congressmen, mayors, etc. visited our church. The mayor addressed us on one occasion, and choking back the tears, said, "You are the first people I've known who've prayed for me!"

In four years, the church grew from 125 to almost 300. We settled into a lovely home. This seemed like a place where we could minister many years.

As in our previous church, one key man, this time Brother Sam,* wanted my assistant pastor fired. The reason—he didn't like him. Sometimes it's Okay to give in. But no leader can compromise his deep convictions of God's will and Christian principles. I did not give in.

The church gave very little to missions. So we scheduled a missionary guest every three to four months. One Sunday after church, Brother Sam exploded in the lobby, "If that preacher has another missionary, I'll throw up!" A group of members and visitors looked at him, stunned.

Each Sunday at 12 noon sharp, two of the deacon's wives pushed out of their pews. They glared at me before going to chat in the lobby. The services usually lasted until 12:15. One day the two jumped me. "You are the most inconsiderate pastor we've ever had!" I was speechless for once. "You hold the services until 12:15, so the Baptists get ahead of us every Sunday at the cafeteria!" This did give me a tip-off concerning their spiritual values.

Now Brother Sam began to phone frequently, sometimes yelling at me over some trivial detail. Then he told me it was time for me to leave. The church had more than doubled, but was not moving fast enough. He snarled, "You know someone else could do better!" Unfortunately, some in leadership can bring about self-fulfilling prophecies, as in this case. As this man started stirring strife, God's Spirit was quenched, and the growth slowed. Visitors came to me to ask if there was trouble in the church. They could sense the unrest.

One morning I felt I had to act. Brother Sam now was on a crusade. He boasted, "80% of the church wants you gone!" Sure, this hurt. I loved the people. Many had been saved and had come into the church during our four years. Without telling anyone, one Sunday I gave everyone a small, blank slip of paper. I reminded the church that I was elected indefinitely. But I simply wanted to know if they were happy with my leadership by just writing "yes" or "no" on the slips of paper. I tried to act casual, and asked that the replies be left on the communion table.

You might guess I was pretty stressed. But in spite of this, God gave us a wonderful service. At the close, the altars were filled with people earnestly seeking the

Lord. As I stepped off the platform, I reached for the "ballots." Suddenly Brother Sam pushed aside those praying and grabbed the papers out of my hand! (One man who got bumped exclaimed, "It's getting right dangerous to pray at the altar these days!")

Now things had come to a head. There was no choice but to call the other six deacons into an emergency meeting. We found Brother Sam in a room studying and counting the responses. As I watched, the color drained from his face. In spite of his dedicated efforts to run us off, only 20% agreed with him. Brother Sam was stunned, and for the first time in his life, speechless and humbled. God's hit man had taken a severe blow. It was time for me to just watch and listen. He searched for words. "I guess I'll have to leave the church!" he said. I could barely hold back a "Hallelujah!" Then he continued, "But you know, I give more money than anyone else." Money and control are partners. And looking at his six bewildered deacon friends, he stated, "And if I leave, many will leave with me."

This was a day I had dreaded. Irreparable damage had been done by this man. Next I turned to the other deacons. "Men, you've observed all the trouble Brother Sam has caused in recent months. And you've watched the fiasco this morning at the altar in our sanctuary. So what should we do?" Their reaction would determine our future ministry.

Each man was given a chance to speak. One by one they shared past experiences. "Oh, Brother Sam, when I was going through a financial struggle, you helped me." Another man chimed in,"We couldn't get along without you." Still another added,"When I was in the hospital, you came to pray."

All the men were this man's friends. But it takes deep character to separate personality from principle. Brother Sam knelt, and, with tears, asked for forgiveness. Unfortunately, the tears were not sincere.

Still, I hoped that somehow things could turn around. The final straw was an application for church membership by two of a district leader's children, close friends of Brother Sam. Attached to the application was a lengthy signed note with a stinging criticism of my ministry. Applications for membership were to be reviewed by the pastor and deacon board. I suggested we decline acceptance of these two, based on their hostility toward the pastor. Why invite trouble? Yet two of the deacons were close friends of the district leader, and said we must accept them. Now I knew my days were numbered, as I would never accept someone into membership who had signed a pledge to serve in harmony, while at the same time including a letter calling for my resignation.

There was one final option left that might solve the dilemma. I met the district leader and showed him the two letters from his children, minus their signatures. I asked his advice. "If you were the pastor, Brother Dean*, and these two wanted to join your church, but in their notes they desired your resignation, what would you do?"

He cleared his throat. "Brother Burgess, you have a real problem."

"I do," I agreed. "But Brother Dean, these letters are from your own kids!" I requested that he counsel with them and point out that one man was manipulating them. I warned him that they could get hurt. This did not seem to concern him, and he refused to speak to his own children about their attitude. I was amazed that a key leader avoided making decisions based on what was right.

Now it was certain—the U-Haul truck would certainly visit our happy home. In my farewell message, one member stood up and demanded, "We want to know why you're resigning." And then he added, "If we don't know why you're resigning, this will happen again and again." His question was appropriate, but I declined to tell of all that had happened behind the scenes.

Two years after our departure, we were invited back to preach the Homecoming. Brother Sam chose not to attend. But we had a wonderful day. Unfortunately, the confusion in the church had continued and the attendance had dwindled. Then the pastor called me aside and demanded, "Why didn't you tell me what was going on? Why didn't you tell me what I'd face here?"

"For one reason, you didn't ask my opinion. And secondly, I hoped things might change," I answered. All I could think of is a favorite saying, "What many churches need is a true revival (not simply getting slain in the Spirit, but of true repentance), or about two funerals."

*Name Change

Back Near Memphis: Munford

Next we were invited to a church close to my hometown of Memphis, Tennessee. The congregation had gotten beaten up in a pastoral change, and we'd been beaten up also. So our ministry there seemed ideal. They had been extremely patient with a previous pastor who was highly gifted, but had offended many of the people. His departure had been tumultuous.

For five years, we enjoyed total bliss. As inconceivable as it seemed, after a few years we still received 100% vote of confidence. The church grew, and was probably the most influential in the area. Yet, one great success there led to a catastrophe. I asked myself and the people, "What ministry would Jesus start if He came to our area?" The obvious answer seemed to be a Christian day care, since that was a need in our area.

I promised the board that we'd find a capable, highly qualified day care director. Then I could be free to pastor and not be involved in the center. It was amazing! The center grew from 5 to 110 students in a matter of months. This required more staff and equipment.

But despite many successes, there were some problems. The monthly financial records submitted to us at times seemed confused, and were always late. And there were some bookkeeping errors. Then the director became ill and was absent for days. Those who took charge during that time found that financial records were either incomplete or not available for auditing. Finally, I insisted on a full audit. In a drawer, we discovered a large number of unpaid bills. The director was an excellent leader, but not gifted in financial management. As pastor, I had to accept the ultimate responsibility.

Soon, another day care center opened in our area. Their nicer and newer facilities attracted some of our staff members and children. We had to lay off some of our staff as attendance dropped. Things started to come unglued. The whole day care operation became an irritant to many of the people at church.

The time came for church deacon board elections. Two board members declined to let their name stand for the coming year. New men joined the leadership, and the dynamics of the deacon board changed. Fresh faces in leadership can either be a blessing or a curse.

Our meetings were no longer harmonious. At the same time, we were considering the future of the church. Space on the current property was limited, and a move to a nearby highway seemed the logical alternative. I spent hours praying and searching for an appropriate site. God in His goodness directed us to 30 prime acres for a low price of $60,000 right on US Highway 51. Over 90% of the church voted to buy the property. But a year later, most voted against making any improvements to it.

By now, a core of good people truly felt it was time for us to go. In our eight years, the church had grown from 175 to about 300. The missions giving had grown from $40,000 to nearly $100,000 a year. The new property was paid for in only two years and we were out of debt.

Unfortunately, some unpleasant things were said and done by people who felt they needed another pastor. It had been our goal to lead the church until our retirement, and then to see our capable assistant take charge. Those who did not want us to leave suggested we start another church in the area—in other words, split the church. For us, this was not an option. So we resigned. Our hearts were broken. We had loved these people. Yet, as in the other two cases, it would only have hurt the Kingdom of God to reveal all the unpleasantness that led to our departure.

You may ask what the point is in sharing sad events. Well, details, both good and bad, tell who a person is. Hopefully, the unpleasant events make us better and not bitter. Also, you may have no idea of the pressures pastors face. Many ministers and their wives and children have been wounded. A host of them today are out of the ministry and bitter. Many church people have been disillusioned by church trouble. So the point is, be careful of folks causing division, and let's be agents for healing and harmony.

Reconciliation—God's Will

Fast forward five years. Two of the most influential leaders in the Munford church were very dear friends. But a vocal minority influenced them. Unfortunately, this brought us into direct conflict. The pain went deep for me. Honestly, I don't think either of them knew how deeply their words hurt. Maybe after 40 years in full-time ministry my skin should be thicker.

After my resignation, I did not speak to them for five years. Sometime I imagined writing a letter of reconciliation. Other times I tossed in bed thinking of how I could give them a piece of my mind. But since I don't have much to spare, that wasn't a very good idea!

In March of 2004, I attended the annual District Council in Nashville. Things ran rather smoothly. But Superintendent Eddie Turner announced a surprise speaker. An out-of-state guest was flying in between other meetings. For 45 minutes he talked about reconciliation. Especially, he focused on the pain pastors endure during church conflicts. Pastors were the majority of those in attendance. The guest spoke candidly about the turmoil and pain he had endured in his ministry. He shared the bliss of letting it go.

Then I saw him. Just in front of me was one of the men from our previous pastorate. He was the one I had loved like a brother. Whether intentionally or not he became "God's hit man." Our guest stated, "There may be people who have hurt you. And you may walk a block just so you don't have to speak."

Then it hit me: just a week earlier I was in Lowe's in Bartlett. As I approached the checkout counter, there stood my adversary. I hate to admit it, but I walked around the entire store to miss him. No it wasn't right, but the wound in my spirit was still sensitive after five years. God had sent this speaker for me; it was time to let go. I was the first one to the altar. All the bitterness and pain poured out of my soul. I arose in peace, the weight was gone!

But it wasn't over. As I returned to my seat, I saw Bob*. Should I turn away, or ignore him, or was this the time to settle it? Sometimes we dream of all the things we might say. But as I approached him, I just threw my arms around his neck. Our tears flowed freely. Beside him was his lovely wife. I don't know how much she knew, but we embraced and prayed for each other.

Only God could have mended this relationship. Of course, we must cooperate. Our fellowship has been restored. The love and mutual respect are evident again.

Now only one nagging question. Was our departure from that church God's will? At the time it was the deepest pain I had ever experienced. But the church there is moving ahead now. And a door has opened for us to minister in Bartlett. We have witnessed a true resurrection of that church that many thought impossible. And in reality, the last five years in Bartlett have been some of the happiest and most productive in our 45 years of ministry. At times Romans 8:28 sounds like a cruel joke: "And we know that in all things God works for the good of those who love him, who have been called according to his purpose" (NIV). His words are true if we just hold steady. As we look back, we realize that God wants our entire lives to be "sponsored by the Holy Spirit!"

*Name Change

39

BARTLETT RESURRECTION

Someone said, "When you're 60, you need a brand new challenge." But there's one minor problem for pastors: most churches want a man who is 32, with an MA degree and 15 years of experience. Today most churches will not consider a man over 55 unless they've had a younger man who was disruptive.

Someone told us about a church in suburban Memphis—Bartlett First Assembly. Due to a crisis, the church had dwindled to around 30. Several churches invited us for interviews, but nothing clicked. And even though I had been told the Bartlett situation was grim, I felt I should at least pray about it. As we met with the deacons, their discouragement was evident. Surprisingly, I felt a strong desire to minister to these hurting people. They warned us they could not guarantee our salary, but promised to do their best. That was all we expected. In the natural, it seemed possible that we would go bankrupt and lose our home. We prepared to put it on the market. That never became necessary, and the church has taken good care of us from the beginning.

I became the worship leader, announcement maker and preacher. Heather became the secretary-bookkeeper, youth pastor and choir leader. Someone said, "Gene, you sure took a big chance going to Bartlett." I joked that there was only one way for things to go, and that was up! When you know you're in God's will, there's nothing to worry about. When someone asked me about my goal for that first year, I replied, "Survival!" We had few programs. All the church could offer was love for God, God's Word, and love for each other. Also, we had a dependence on the Holy Spirit. In reality, these are the most essential anyhow.

How I thank God for a core of people who stayed faithful in the troubled times before our arrival. If they had not remained, the church would have closed. An attendance of 75 seemed an impossible goal. I remember calling my mom, Mildred Hamill, the day we reached 100 in attendance.

Now as we enter in our sixth year, more than 250 call Bartlett First Assembly of God home. We have dedicated, capable leadership in every area of ministry.

My dear friend and assistant, Sam Tollison, is not only my right hand, but part of my left hand too. His wife Amy is invaluable.

On our arrival, if someone had told us that in five years we would start construction on a $1.3 million, 10,000 sq. ft. Family Life/Worship Center, I may have run. A building program is not one of my favorite challenges. Our goal was never to have a bigger church, but to be a lighthouse to reach our community. But as we grew, I shared my deep conviction with the people, "If we do not build, attendance will level off when the building is comfortably full. We will stagnate, and people will drift away. So the main thing is not what we want, but what God wants." This vision gradually gripped the hearts of our leaders, and they voted to move forward.

Our people were already giving generously. Some thought if we could raise $100,000 over a three-year period, or even $200,000, for the new building over our normal offerings, we would be doing exceedingly well. When our pledges reached nearly $300,000, the excitement was electric! A member of the building committee and a general contractor, John Reinagel, volunteered to do the building at a cost of just 3% for oversight and project management. We were astounded at the offer.

The Lord had brought to my side willing, capable people. Many have felt God specifically leading them to join in this spiritual adventure at Bartlett First Assembly. Each has helped put steel in the foundation of the ministry. In fact, our next goal is not 200 members, but 200 ministers. When someone commented, "Everyone at that church thinks they're ministers," all I could say was, "Praise the Lord."

Now as we pause at this point in our ministry and look back, we thank God for all the people who have assisted us, prayed for us, supported us, and encouraged us. And we realize that all that has been accomplished is because this ministry was "sponsored by the Holy Spirit."

978-0-595-35410-8
0-595-35410-6

Printed in the United States
31457LVS00004B/82-123